09-BTO-382

The Witness
of
the Worshiping Community

Liturgy and the Practice of Evangelism

Frank C. Senn

PAULIST PRESS
New York/Mahwah, N.J.

Library of Congress Cataloging-in-Publication Data

Senn, Frank C.
    The witness of the worshiping community/by Frank C. Senn.
      p. cm.
    Includes bibliographical references.
    ISBN 0-8091-3368-7
    1. Public worship. 2. Evangelistic work. 3. Liturgics.
    I. Title.
    BV15.S46   1993
    264—dc20   92-34033
                                                CIP

Published by Paulist Press
997 Macarthur Boulevard
Mahwah, New Jersey 07430

Printed and bound in the
United States of America

Contents

111400

DEDICATED TO

THE LITURGICAL CONFERENCE

on the occasion of

its Fiftieth Anniversary

1942–1992

Preface

My introduction both to the study of liturgy and to the study of Christian mission was the little book written in 1963 for the National Student Christian Federation by the Russian Orthodox theologian, Alexander Schmemann (now of blessed memory), *For the Life of the World.* That book ignited my interest in Christian liturgy; but it should be recognized that this book was really a theology of mission from a liturgical perspective. That is, the worship of the church was viewed as both the source and the goal of evangelism.

Those who are members of the so-called "liturgical churches," in which historical and theological norms have governed the practice of public worship, have sometimes perceived a gap between what is done in these churches "out of the book" and the religiously unlettered who are invited into these churches. This has created a certain tension because these churches want to reach out with the gospel to the unchurched. On the other hand, the historic liturgy embodies the beliefs of the community of faith in Jesus Christ crucified, dead, and risen again, and the adoration and praise of the triune God, to which we want to initiate those who respond to the invitation to identify with the fellowship of the gospel. "Initiation" should really be the operative concept here which bridges this gap. It is the arduous task of making Christians which perhaps

1

the contemporary American church lacks the will or the skill to perform.

Americans look for the "quick fix," and that may be one way to explain the appeal of the "church growth" movement to the problem of evangelism. If the liturgy of the church represents a reality which is opaque to the casual Sunday morning visitor, then it should be more accessible to the uninitiated. Church growth seminars advertise "Worship that attracts and holds the unchurched." Modest changes to facilitate this appeal to the unchurched include printing out the whole order of service so that worshipers don't have to fumble with a cumbersome worship book. But with the help of word processors this leads easily to amending texts and deleting parts of the liturgy that seem inscrutable to the uninformed. More major changes include abandoning liturgical forms altogether in favor of a free order devoid of liturgical accoutrements and vestments. More radical departures include proposals of "entertainment evangelism" which entice people to church on Sunday mornings with promises of fun and frolic and an upbeat message to help people get through the week. In some of these churches the congregation never gets so deep into the Christian faith as to confess the Apostles' Creed or pray the Lord's Prayer. The sermon, delivered away from a podium by an unvested preacher with softcover Bible in hand, is on a topic that is unrelated to any text. The upbeat music is performed by a combo on the stage with virtually no congregational participation. There are no acts of devotion to God other than putting money in the collection plates. It is a mystery that anyone could regard this as either worship or evangelism. It is certainly not "church" since there is no assembly for the word of God and the sacraments of Christ.

These "church growth" oriented parishes, often styled "community churches" so as not to turn off potential attendees with doctrinaire-sounding confessional tags, claim to take seriously the task of initiating the unchurched into the faith. This is done through a kind of catechetical process which leads to participation in a "liturgy of the faithful" on Wednesday or some other night, but absolutely not on Sunday morning. Thus the Lord's day is given over to those who do not yet confess themselves to be a part of the Lord's people.

There is a vague correlation between this pattern and the initiation practices of the ancient church. Catechumens did not gain immediate access to the liturgy of the faithful. They attended a liturgy of the word and received instruction leading to baptism before they could participate in the eucharist. Even the preaching at these public services of the word was geared toward a varied public; instruction in the mysteries of the faith (i.e., the sacraments) was withheld until after baptism and first communion. However, a solidly established fellowship and liturgy of the faithful existed into which the neophytes could be incorporated. This incorporation was the clear goal of Christian initiation, and the processes of initiation were long and arduous. But the church's energies were directed toward building up the eucharistic fellowship, not toward celebrational encounters with the unchurched.

I am not sufficiently prophetic to perceive whether the "church growth movement" represents a tidal wave or a ripple in the history of Christian mission. Nor am I above gleaning insights from this movement, which has taught us to pay attention to the needs and concerns of the vast numbers of unchurched people in our country. It has prompted us to reconsider our practices of hospitality to strangers. This book is neither a critique nor an appreciation of the "church growth movement." But it is written out of concern that many of those in mainline churches, both in parishes and in the denominational staffs, are buying into principles of the "church growth move-ment" in a seemingly last-ditch effort to stem membership hemorrhaging.

This book is written in the conviction that there needs to be a more secure connection between liturgy and evan-gelism; that worship in word and sacrament should be re-garded as a part of the mission of God and not just as some-thing that aids the church in mission; that missionary dimensions are implicit in the celebration of the sacra-ments; that the central symbols of bathing and dining call attention to our practices of hospitality and raise the issue of inculturation of the liturgy; and that churches which take seriously the liturgy as their primary form of public witness need to develop a liturgical evangelism. That kind of evangelism will take the form of Christian initiation of adults and children with whom the congregation has be-gun a relationship.

I have had occasion to address these issues in bits and pieces over the last several years in different settings, in-cluding conferences, workshops, seminars, and a synod as-sembly. The urgency of dealing with the issue of the rela-tionship between liturgy and mission, worship and evangelism, has spurred me on to find the time (an hour here, a few minutes there) to commit these convictions to written form and to share them with a wider circle of col-leagues in ministry and congregational life. My thanks to the publishing house of the Missionary Society of St. Paul for their willingness to disseminate this witness to the wider church.

During the Time after the Epiphany
Immanuel Lutheran Church
Evanston, Illinois 1992

Worship and Witness: Tensions and Relationships

Two of the most important things the church does are to *worship* the God and Father of our Lord Jesus Christ and to *witness* to God's mighty acts of creation, redemption, and sanctification. This little book is a study of the interrelation between worship and witness. We have called it *The Witness of the Worshiping Community.* This is to indicate that we are concerned to reflect on the role of the worshiping community in the mission of God.

One would think that there is an interconnection between everything the church does, but that is not always apparent. J. G. Davies wrote a book, *Worship and Mission,* because there has been a tendency to understand worship *inwardly,* as that which builds up the body of Christ, rather than *outwardly,* in terms of mission.[1] This book picks up Davies' concern but modifies it to indicate ways in which worship is itself an aspect of the mission of God.

We need to begin with a vocabulary study, because language is a reflection of our notional concepts and also helps to form them. "Worship" comes from the old Anglo-Saxon word *weorthscripe,* which means "to ascribe worth." It was not necessarily a religious word in origin. Indeed, to this day magistrates in Britain are addressed as "your worship." The word connotes creature-feelings of awe and reverence, of honor and respect. Worship is something we instinctively do as human creatures. So far as we know, the human is the only *praying* animal. The "fall" has not obliterated humankind's religious instincts. Indeed, the essential problem of Christian life is not to engage in religious activities, but to perceive and acknowledge God's lordship over the totality of life. In this sense, "worship" is an attitude and activity which occurs both within and outside of the cultic community, because one renders honor to God in one's ethical conduct as well as in one's offering of prayer, praise, and thanksgiving. We shall see that this is also true of the Greek New Testament's word for "worship," *latreia.*

It is also true of another term which has been used to designate the activity which we usually call "worship"—"liturgy." The term *leitourgia* (from *leiton,* "pertaining to the people," and *ergon,* "work"—hence, "the work of the people") is used in the New Testament to refer both to the worship of the church (Acts 13:2) and to the collecting of funds for the relief of the poor in Jerusalem (2 Cor 9:12). *Leitourgia* is the work or service that an individual or group performs on behalf of others. The church has ministers who render liturgy to the community, and the community of faith as a whole renders liturgy on behalf of the world. It is noteworthy that both the terms *leitourgia* and *diakonia* can be translated as "ministry," which suggests a relationship between performing a service on behalf of others and rendering assistance to others.

"To witness" is to tell what one knows. It comes from the Anglo-Saxon word *witan,* "to know" (from which we derive the word "wit"). It is to attest to a fact, to give evidence of a reality. The witness tells what he or she has heard, seen, or otherwise experienced. We shall be suggesting that the cultic arena in which God's word is proclaimed and the sacraments of Christ are administered is a

6

source of the experience of God to which the Christian bears witness.

"Evangelism" is a term which has been used to designate the activity of witnessing. It has at its root the Greek term *evangelion*, which means "good news" in its broad sense, and "gospel" as a book dealing with the life and teachings of Jesus in the narrow sense. We can define "evangel*ism*" as spreading good news—witnessing to what God has done in Jesus the Christ. Those with good news to share are those with a "mission." "Mission" also has a broad and a narrow sense. It derives from the Latin *mittere*, "to send," and in the narrow sense refers to sending out persons to preach, to teach, and to proselytize. Hence we speak of "missionaries." In the broad sense "mission" refers to the special task or purpose a person or a group has. In this sense worship is as much a part of the church's mission as evangelism or social ministry. The terms "mission" or "missionary" do not appear in the New Testament. Their Greek equivalents would be *apostello*, "to send out," and *apostolos* (apostle), "a sent one" in the sense of an ambassador or messenger. It's not uncommon to find the term "apostolate" used in Roman Catholic literature where Protestant literature would use the term "mission."

It is apparent that there is some overlapping of meanings when these terms are broadly understood. We are considering the witness of the worshiping community. It is obvious that worship is an act of witness. Martin Luther understood this, and for this reason he suggested that communicants gather in the chancel to receive holy communion—so that they could be seen by those who were not receiving the sacrament, and could thereby witness to the others by their lives and actions. Pastors and lay leaders are well aware of the fact that a full church makes a more positive impression on visitors than a half-empty or half-full church. Just getting up on Sunday mornings and

7

going to church makes a witness to friends, relatives, and neighbors. Testimony to the gospel by one's actions as well as one's words is also a way of ascribing worth to God.

Nevertheless, worship and witness more narrowly understood seem to be oriented in different directions. Worship is more narrowly understood to be an activity which nourishes the members of the church, whereas witness is commonly regarded as reaching out to persons who are not members. This kind of outreach is usually proselytism, which is trying to convince someone to embrace the beliefs and practices of a particular community. Proselytism is a defective understanding and practice of evangelism which I will take up in chapter 3. The point I am making here is that those who give leadership to nurture and those who give leadership to outreach are frequently oriented in different directions and usually develop different kinds of concerns and skills. Congregational worship and music and evangelism and social ministry committees seldom meet together. This lack of cross-fertilization between worship and evangelism, and between the disciplines of liturgiology and missiology, also occurs in denominational program staffs and theological seminary faculties. Those who make worship the object of specialized study scarcely ever consider the witness of the worshiping community, and those who are concerned to develop a theology and practice of evangelism seem to have little interest in cultic acts except to fine-tune them into evangelistic tools. Only recently, in consideration of the problems of cultural indigenization, have liturgiologists and missiologists found a common ground for meeting. Crises do tend to bring people together.

Disunity between worship and witness therefore seems to be characteristic of contemporary Christian life and thought, and yet this is entirely contrary to the outlook that is found in the New Testament and the early church. In the apostolic writings, the life and work of

Christ are spoken of in terms of both mission and cultic life. In John 12:49 we read: "For I have not spoken on my own authority; the Father who *sent* me has himself given me commandment what to say and what to speak." In John 6:51 cultic language is applied to Jesus' mission or apostolate: "I am the living bread which comes down from heaven; if anyone eats of this bread, he will live forever; and the bread which I shall give for the life of the world is my flesh." The dimensions of mission and sacramental life are joined together in verse 57: "As the living Father *sent* me, and I live because of the Father, so he who *eats* me will live because of me." This unity of inward life and outward mission is also evident in the specific New Testament and patristic terms for "worship" and "witness," *latreia* and *martyria*.

Latreia can mean the liturgical rites instituted by God and regulated by the laws of the Old Covenant. Paul uses the term in this way in Romans 9:4. Also in Hebrews 9:1 and 6 the term is applied to the official acts of the priest in the tabernacle or in the temple. However, where *latreia* is used in the New Testament to refer to what Christians do, it conveys an entirely different meaning; for Christians are told by Paul that their *latreia* is a "spiritual worship"—the undivided surrender of their entire physical existence to God (Rom 12:1).[2]

This complete surrender to God—presenting one's body as a "living sacrifice"—is required by the eschatological situation in which Christians find themselves. As we read in Hebrews 9:14, the sacrifice of Christ has served to "purify your conscience from dead works to serve the living God" ("to serve" = *latreuein*). At the same time, Christians are conscious of the grave nearness of the day of judgment when all people will be confronted by the God who will prove himself to be a consuming fire in his judgment; so they are filled with gratitude and awe. "Therefore let us be grateful for receiving a kingdom that cannot be

9

shaken, and thus let us offer to God acceptable worship, with reverence and awe; for our God is a consuming fire" (Heb 12:28–29).

In Philippians 3 Paul emphasizes the fact that Christians find themselves in a new situation, a new reality brought about by the death and resurrection of Jesus the Christ. Therefore he warns the congregation: "Look out for the dogs, look out for the evil-workers, look out for those who mutilate the flesh. For we are the true circumcision, who worship God in spirit, and glory in Christ Jesus, and put no confidence in the flesh" (Phil 3:2–3). Worship here designates the total conduct of the Christian before God. This conduct is made feasible and is effected solely through the miraculous gift of the messianic end-time: the Spirit of God. But the Spirit has burst asunder the legal-ritual bonds to the Torah and its specific forms of worship. The Spirit touches the whole of human life. Therefore, to serve God in the Spirit through this *latreia* must indeed be the Christians' "living sacrifice" described in Romans 12:1.

There is no doubt that there was a kind of ritual bareness in the worship of the early Christians. This should not be taken merely as a sign of primitiveness; the early Christians were not primitive people; most of them were sophisticated or at least street-wise urban dwellers. They had come from backgrounds in the highly ritualized (or perhaps we should say highly ceremonialized) pagan and Jewish cults. But they were at pains to stress the difference between their "reasonable sacrifice" (*logike thusia*) and the highly ritualized worship of the pagans and Jews. Minucius Felix, writing at the end of the second century, asked the Roman authorities:

> Do you think we hide the object of our worship because we have no shrines or altars? What image am I to contrive of God, since logical reasoning tells you that

10

man himself is an image of God? What temple am I to build for him, since this whole world, fashioned by his hand, cannot hold him? Am I to confine so vast and majestic a power to one little shrine, while I, a mere man, live in a larger place? Are our mind and heart not better places to be dedicated to him?[3]

It is evident that the very *style* of Christian worship made a witness to the revealed truth, and it was a style purposely out-of-sync with other worship styles which flourished in the Greco-Roman culture. The actual form of Christian worship matches this defense of ritual bareness, as it is given to us by Justin Martyr in chapter 67 of his *First Apology* (ca. 150 A.D.). He relates that on Sunday Christians come together in one place to celebrate the resurrection of Christ. They read from the prophetic and apostolic writings, and the president comments on these readings. Then they pray for people according to their needs and exchange the kiss of peace. Then bread and a cup of wine mixed with water are brought to the president, and he gives thanks over them to the best of his ability. The deacons then distribute the consecrated bread and wine and take the sacramental elements to the absent. Those who are able make contributions, and the president takes care of those who are in want.

An elaboration of the Christian cult began to occur at the beginning of the third century in reaction to the threat of heresies. Written prayer formularies appear, at least as models for the presiding ministers. To counter the Gnostic devaluation of the material creation, the bread and wine are actually offered in an offertory procession of the whole congregation of the faithful. As a consequence the name of the liturgy of the Lord's supper, which had been *eucharistia* ("thanksgiving") in the early centuries, became *oblatio* ("offering") in the third and fourth centuries.

Still, this was nothing compared with the elaboration

of the Christian cult which occurred in the fourth and fifth centuries, in the wake of the conversion of the emperor Constantine, the legalization of the Christian cult by the Edict of Milan in 313, the restitution of church property confiscated during the times of persecution, the increasing favoritism shown toward the church by the imperial government, and the hordes of people seeking membership in the church as a result of that favoritism. Alexander Schmemann, the great Orthodox liturgiologist and theologian (now of blessed memory), suggested that the history of Christian worship at this time can be reduced to the following basic processes:

> (1) the development and complication of the external ceremonial of worship, related at first to the building of churches; (2) the increasing complication of liturgical "cycles"--the Church Year, the week and the day; the appearance of new feasts or whole festal cycles, new liturgical days and new services; (3) the rapid growth of hymnody, which gradually became the main element of worship; and finally (4) the extraordinary development of the Sanctoral—the reverencing of the tombs of the saints, relics, etc.[4]

If we analyze each one of these developments, we can see that the seeds of each were already planted in the pre-Constantinian church. So it was not a matter of exchanging one kind of worship for another. Schmemann suggested that it was in the area of piety or spirituality that a real revolution occurred. The church had a herculean task of absorbing and forming in the faith the masses of converts coming into the church during the fourth and fifth centuries. These people brought with them a pagan mindset that there is a gap between the sacred and the profane, and the purpose of the cult is to bridge that gap. Christianity had been preached as a saving faith in the early centuries, not as a saving cult. But the masses of converts coming into the church during the fourth and fifth centuries viewed ritual performance itself as efficacious. There is no doubt that Christian worship took on more of the characteristics of the cult-dramas performed in the popular mystery cults in which the saving event is repeated or reactualized in the dramatic imitations of the rites. During this time we find the liturgy taking on more of the characteristics of dramatic imitation of the events in the life, death, resurrection, and ascension of Jesus. Or else the actions of the liturgy were interpreted as representing these events in an allegorical sense.

Now, to be sure, the biblical concept of "remembrance" (anamnesis) has the sense of experiencing anew the unique events of salvation history. In the Christian cult this was accomplished by the presence of the Spirit of the risen Christ bringing to the "remembrance" of Jesus' followers all that he had said and done so that these could be appropriated by the Spirit's gift of faith. But the converts saw this happening in the performance of the rites. The dramatic quality of liturgy has proven to have an enduring attraction for people. This can be seen not only in Palm Sunday processions and footwashing ceremonies, but also in "living nativity scenes" and passion plays. The problem is that in the west, with its developed historical consciousness, this can be very theologically limiting. For example, the current fad of celebrating the Lord's supper on Maundy Thursday in the context of an actual Jewish Passover seder reduces the Lord's supper to the last supper of Jesus and his disciples, whereas for the early church it was the foretaste of the messianic feast in the kingdom of God, in which the crucified and risen messiah was present, giving himself to his faithful followers. The Lord's supper is not an historical reenactment, it is an eschatological event in which the future sheds new light on the past as well as transforming the present.

It was precisely this sense of the inauguration of the

future kingdom of God in the midst of the old order of sin and death that was lost because of the church's evangelistic success. Pagan idols could be destroyed, pagan temples could be demolished, pagan sacrifices could be prohibited; but the pagan mindset could not be so easily eradicated. This mindset regarded the cult as serving the purpose of saving devotees from the contaminations of the world, whereas the Christian gospel had been proclaimed as God's act in Jesus the Christ for the *salvation of the world.* "God so loved the world *(kosmos)* that he gave his only-begotten Son. . . ." There is no doubt that something of the freshness, vitality, and even the truth of the gospel was lost when the church had to absorb so many new members that it didn't have the time or energy to work for a more complete conversion of each individual one. This lesson from history should warn us that missionary success can result in a loss of the real mission of the church. It has happened many times, and it usually happens right under our noses.

Perhaps for this very reason we need to recover the New Testament's understanding of what it means to bear witness. The word for "witness" in the Greek New Testament is *martyria.* What is a martyr? According to the story of the martyrdom of Stephen in Acts 7, a martyr is a witness to Christ in the midst of suffering. It was as Stephen was being stoned to death that he saw "the heavens opened, and the Son of man standing on the right hand of God" (Acts 7:56). It's no wonder that there was such a desire for martyrdom among the early Christians! This reaches chilling proportions in the letters of Ignatius of Antioch at the beginning of the second century. On his way to Rome in the company of a band of soldiers for almost certain death in the arena, he wrote to the Roman Christians:

> I am corresponding with all the churches and bidding them all realize that I am voluntarily dying for God—

14

if, that is, you do not interfere. I plead with you, do not do me an unseasonable kindness. Let me be fodder for wild beasts—that is how I can get to God. I am God's wheat and I am being ground by the teeth of the wild beasts to make a pure loaf for Christ. I would rather that you fawn on the beasts so that they may be my tomb and no scrap of my body be left. Thus, when I have fallen asleep, I shall be a burden to no one. Then I shall be a real disciple of Jesus Christ when the world sees my body no more. Pray Christ for me that by these means I may become God's sacrifice.[5]

There are several themes which appear in this passage, and which are amplified elsewhere in the letters of Ignatius. One is the longing for eschatological perfection: martyrdom is "how I can get to God." A second theme is the imitation of Christ: martyrdom is how "I shall be a real disciple of Jesus Christ." A third theme is the description of martyrdom in eucharistic terms: "I am God's wheat and I am being ground . . . to make a pure loaf for Christ." Indeed, later in this same letter Ignatius writes, "I take no delight in corruptible food or in the dainties of this life. What I want is God's bread, which is the flesh of Christ, who came from David's line; and for drink I want his blood: an immortal love feast indeed."[6]

It is not surprising that Ignatius speaks about the eucharist frequently in his letters. It is a foretaste of the messianic feast, and therefore an eschatological event. It is a participation in the crucified, risen, and ascended Lord Jesus Christ. Eating and drinking the body and blood of this Christ associates us with his passion and triumph. In the eucharist we receive the seed of what he is; and this seed bears fruit in martyrdom, in witness. All of these implications become explicit in the remarkable *Martyrdom of Polycarp*. The aged bishop prayed a eucharistic prayer at the stake and then, according to the description of the eyewitnesses, became a eucharistic oblation:

15

So they did not nail him, but tied him. And with his hands out behind him and tied, like a noble ram out of a great flock ready for sacrifice, a burnt offering ready and acceptable to God, he looked up to heaven and said:

"Lord God Almighty, Father of they beloved and blessed Servant Jesus Christ, through whom we have received full knowledge of thee, 'the God of angels and powers and all creation' and of the whole race of the righteous who live in thy presence: I bless thee, because thou hast deemed me worthy of this day and hour, to take my part in the number of the martyrs, in the cup of thy Christ; for 'resurrection to eternal life' of soul and body in the immortality of the Holy Spirit; among whom may I be received in thy presence this day as a rich and acceptable sacrifice, just as thou hast prepared and revealed beforehand and fulfilled, thou that art the true God without any falsehood. For this and for everything I praise thee, I bless thee, I glorify thee, through the eternal and heavenly High Priest, Jesus Christ, thy beloved Servant, through whom be glory to thee with him and Holy Spirit both now and unto the ages to come. Amen."

And when he had concluded the Amen and finished his prayer, the men attending to the fire lighted it. And when the flame flashed forth, we saw a miracle, we to whom it was given to see. And we are preserved in order to relate to the rest what happened. For the fire made the shape of a vaulted chamber, like a ship's sail filled by the wind, and made a wall around the body of the martyr. And he was in the midst, not as burning flesh, but as bread baking or as gold and silver refined in a furnace. And we perceived such a sweet aroma as the breath of incense or some other precious spice.[7]

The relation between the eucharist and martyrdom must be understood exactly. Martyrdom was not regarded as a substitute for the eucharist; indeed there were those preparing for martyrdom who would eat nothing except the eucharistic bread. Rather, what is given obscurely veiled in the eucharist is revealed in its stark reality in martyrdom: the presence in us of Christ dead and risen again. It is not surprising, given this certainty, that the early church fathers regarded martyrdom even as a substitute for baptism. Both Tertullian and Hippolytus held that a person who was martyred for the faith before he or she could be baptized would be regarded as having been baptized in his or her own blood. Origen more boldly said, "Only the baptism of blood makes us more pure than the baptism of water."[8] He based this on the words of Jesus in Luke 12:50, "I have a baptism to be baptized with; and how I am constrained until it is accomplished." This baptism referred to Jesus' sacrifice of his life for the life of the world. Again, in his *Exhortation to Martyrdom*, Origen appealed to the words of Jesus to explain martyrdom as the supreme eucharist of the Christian: "Can you drink the cup that I am to drink?" (Mt 20:22) and "Father if it is possible, let this cup pass from me. Nevertheless, not what I will, but what thou wilt" (Mt 26:39).[9]

Naturally, this form of witness was no longer possible once the age of persecution was ended by the Edict of Milan (although there have been Christian martyrs in every age, no more so than in the twentieth century). New forms of witnessing arose in *asceticism*, which was the organization of one's life in conformity with the cross of Christ; in *monasticism*, which was the dedication of one's life to wage warfare against spiritual enemies and to pray for the world; and later in the *mendicant orders* (e.g., the Franciscans), who cultivated an imitation of the poverty of Christ and thereby witnessed to his identification with the least of his brothers and sisters. These movements were efforts to maintain a witness to the eschatological reality that had been inaugurated in the death and resurrection of Christ and the outpouring of his Spirit. This witness was also made by the Anabaptist martyrs and confessors of the

17

sixteenth century, and by those Christians who protested the "worldliness" or "secularization" of the church, such as the Puritans and Pietists. The problem with the puritanical and pietistic reaction to the church's captivity to the powers and spirit of "this world" is that Christians ceased to see "this world" as the arena of their witnessing. Yet there are those Christians who make a real witness to the power of the cross and the resurrection of Christ in the midst of their own suffering. They are true martyrs in that by their words and behavior they indicate that God is their very life: that everything in their life comes from God and must be returned to God. As Schmemann has written in his classic, *For the Life of the World,*

> Here is a man suffering on his bed of pain and the Church comes to him to perform the sacrament of healing. For this man, as for every man in the whole world, suffering can be defeat, the way of complete surrender to darkness, despair and solitude. It can be *dying* in the very real sense of the word. And yet it can also be the ultimate victory of Man and of Life in him. The Church does not come to restore *health* in this man, simply to replace medicine when medicine has exhausted its own possibilities. The Church comes to take this man into the Love, the Light, and the Life of Christ. It comes not merely to "comfort" him in his sufferings, not to "help" him, but to make him a *martyr*, a *witness* to Christ in his very sufferings.[10]

I have devoted this attention to the theme of martyrdom because it is evident that for the New Testament and the early church there was no dichotomy between worship and witness. Both *latreia* and *martyria* partook of the eschatological reality toward which Christian personal and communal life is oriented. It is in the recovery of worship as the celebration of the kingdom of God and of witness as testimony to the inauguration of the kingdom that worship and witness among us can be reunited as aspects of the same mission of the church. But the task is not just to reunite them and then to assume that each will correct the other; for both worship and witness have suffered distortions by forces outside themselves. A particular example of this is to be found in Pietism. Worship, under the influence of Pietism—especially in the late nineteenth century —became preoccupied with the individual rather than with the community. It became focused on the *response* of people to the action of God rather than on the celebration and proclamation of the mighty acts of God. This is especially evident in the practices of revivalism. The revivalists knew, along with their counterparts in the commerce and industry of pragmatic, optimistic American society, that there was no limit to what could be accomplished if the right techniques were used. If the theology of revivalism was weak (for example, dividing all humanity into the saved and the damned), its understanding of human behavior was profound. Revivalists knew how to elicit from people the kind of response they desired and directed preaching and singing toward this end. Worship was focused on the human response rather than on the praise and adoration of God.[11] The revivalists' concept of evangelism was to "save" the individual, not to announce the good news of God's saving work in Jesus Christ to the world.

The church growth movement is a modern form of revivalism, utilizing the sophisticated techniques of communications theory and practice in order to package and market forms of church life designed to appeal to certain types of people. Like revivalism, it stresses the personal appeal of the gospel rather than its public proclamation. "Church Growth, Inc." of Monrovia, California holds one-day leadership seminars around the country on "Worship That Attracts and Holds the Unchurched." It does not hold up one style of worship that can be analyzed, but rather examines "how worship and church growth are inter-related, what is the mind-set of Americans in the 1990s, and how worship can be a tool for new outreach and growth for your church.''[12] The Community Church of Joy (Evangelical Lutheran Church in America) of Phoenix, Arizona, holds an annual four-day conference which, in 1991, included among its evangelism workshops (which are impressive in their range and scope): resources for dynamic music and worship. The idea is that there are contemporary worship and music styles that will meet people, especially the "baby boomers," where they are. But the worship style that results from the marketing approach to liturgy and evangelism would probably not prompt a child to ask, as the child does at the Jewish Passover Seder, "Why are we doing this? Why is this night different from every other night?" The question would not be asked because there is nothing "odd" about such liturgies. They are not out of step with the world and therefore they cannot present a real alternative to the world's claims.[13]

One thing the old revivalists had right was that there is a need for conversion—for a change from one mode of existence to another. We cannot ignore where our prospective or present Christians are coming from. The impact of secularism on our common life and the way it has marginalized religious commitment must be taken seriously. Television plays a major role in creating our culture, and nothing on commercial television does anything to encourage going to church, reading the Bible, or exploring faith in God. Furthermore, our marginalized religious life is tied to the peculiar tradition of individualism in American society which is so well chronicled by Robert Bellah and his associates in *Habits of the Heart*.[14] The individualism which is under attack in this study is not the healthy development of a differentiated self, but rather the private view of the "pursuit of happiness" that has no interest in raising questions concerning the common good. In fact, this individualism may be exacerbated by the weariness with the

20

political process that has set in as a result of the failure of the hopes for a renewed society ignited in the 1960s. "Conversion" in this context can only mean a reorientation of one's sensibilities and values; and there is some concern about whether the contemporary American church is up to the task.

The problem of presenting a Christian challenge and alternative to our secular society is not helped by the worship and evangelism styles and techniques proposed by the church growth movement. There is no doubt that these techniques are sophisticated and successful. Many of them are applications learned from the success of televangelism. The most successful televangelists (e.g., Jerry Falwell, Pat Robertson, Robert Schuller, Jimmy Swaggart) have moved beyond the old revivalists in learning how to target an audience. The older evangelists such as Bishop Fulton J. Sheen and Dr. Billy Graham had already learned how to make use of the electronic media in pursuit of the Great Commission. What the new generation of televangelists understand is the need to cultivate TV personalities and to keep the message simple and appealing. In a recent book on televangelism, Quentin J. Schultze observes that "God does not play well on television. Spirited televangelists do, and they offer the kind of authority that parish pastors seem to lack."[15] And Neil Postman, in a more far-ranging study of American television as a form of entertainment, including religious broadcasting, wonders if the presentation of the gospel in such a "user-friendly" medium does not actually undermine the gospel. "I believe I am not mistaken in saying that Christianity is a demanding and serious religion. When it is delivered as easy and amusing, it is another kind of religion altogether."[16]

Worship done under the auspices of church growth has picked up on the entertainment factor in successful televangelism. In fact, Pastor Walter Kallesatad of the Community Church of Joy, Phoenix, speaks of "entertain-

21

ment evangelism."[17] Quentin Schultze observes that "Across the Protestant and Roman Catholic spectrum, local congregational worship seems more and more like a Hollywood production." While noting that TV is not the only influence on contemporary worship, Schultze observes that: "The key words used by advocates are 'relaxed,' 'informal,' 'interesting,' and 'relevant,' " with TV-styled services as "the inevitable result."[18]

The problem with entertainment is that it works best when it leaves the people in the audience satisfied—satisfied with themselves and their world. It does not usually plant seeds of self-doubt that lead to a desire for change. It works best when personalities appeal to persons. It does not build up a sense of community. To bring together an individualistic orientation in worship with an individualistic orientation in witness is no great gain for the life and mission of the church as the eschatological community "called out" of the world (ekklesia) in order to herald and model the new life and the new creation in Christ. What we need is a rethinking of both worship and witness in the light of the gospel of the eschatological kingdom of God.

One way to get at this rethinking is to define the character of worship over against some common and well-intended corruptions in practice, and to reconsider the meaning of witness against the background of some defective concepts of evangelism. We will devote the next two chapters to this via negativa. Then, in a more constructive vein, we will take up the two sacraments of baptism and eucharist and explore the missionary dimensions inherent in each of these constitutive acts of God in the church. We shall develop the view that worship in word and sacrament is essentially an encounter between God and God's people, and that it is right to invite others into the arena of this encounter in the worshiping community. We shall take up the practices of hospitality and the concerns for inculturation that must accompany an invitation to come to

22

church. And then, assuming that the invitation is accepted and that those who come are convinced by God's Spirit to identify with the fellowship of the gospel, we shall describe an approach to liturgy and evangelism which unites these two activities in the rigors of Christian initiation through which new Christians are made and the church is built up as a community of witness.

The Character of Worship: Corruptions of Practice

One way to get at the meaning of worship is to analyze what is happening in the liturgy itself. We begin with the fact that the people assemble. In the act of assembling they constitute the church. *Ekklesia* means those who are "called out." The church is those people called out of the world to assemble in the presence of God. What they do in this assembly is their "public work" or *leitourgia.* As a preliminary act the worshipers may engage in a rite of purification in which they confess their sins and hear a word of forgiveness or a declaration of grace. This is done in remembrance of baptism—hence the invocation of the trinitarian name and the sign of the cross, both of which have been placed on the people in holy baptism.

It is noteworthy that contemporary Roman Catholic, Episcopal, Lutheran, United Methodist, and Presbyterian worship orders follow a similar shape. Worship proper begins with an entrance song, a series of petitions with the acclamation "Lord, have mercy," and/or a song of praise. After a greeting from the presiding minister and a brief prayer, the congregation settles down to hear readings from the Bible. These churches now follow a common three-year lectionary of readings. The readings are interspersed with psalmody and an Alleluia heralding the coming of Christ in the gospel. Christ's presence in the gospel is signified by the fact that the people jump to their feet and acclaim him: "Glory to you, O Lord. Praise to you, O Christ." A preacher then expounds on these readings in the context of the liturgical celebration and the situation in which the community and its members find themselves in the world. There is time for reflection, a creedal response, and prayers "for the whole people of God in Christ Jesus, and for all people according to their needs." The intercessions are typically produced locally with an opportunity for members of the assembly to add their own concerns before the prayers are summed up and concluded by the presiding minister.

After the prayers the people greet one another with the words and a gesture of peace, offer material gifts while some of their members sing special music, express their self-offering in a prayer spoken together, and continue to offer praise and thanksgiving over the bread and cup on the altar in remembrance of all that God has done in Christ. This Great Thanksgiving is offered by the presiding minister, but the people interject acclamations— "Holy, holy, holy Lord, God of power and might" . . . "Christ has died. Christ is risen. Christ will come again." . . . "Amen. Come, Lord Jesus,"—and they make this prayer their own by adding their "Amen." They all join in the Lord's Prayer, and then bread and wine are shared among the people while suitable songs and hymns are sung. After the ministration of holy communion there is a brief prayer asking God for the benefits of this sacrament in their lives, a blessing by the presiding minister, and a dismissal which implies some consequence of having engaged in this liturgy: "Go in peace. Serve the Lord."

We would note that there are several *directions of communication* in this liturgical event. There are words which the people address to God. There are words by which the people are addressed, presumably by God

25

through the means of a human speaker and signs that they receive (e.g., bread and wine). There is also communication by the gathered people to one another in the forms of greetings and dialogue. There is also communication on behalf of people not present in the assembly (e.g., the leaders of church and state, the hospitalized and ill, prisoners and travelers, etc.). There is probably, if we look hard enough, some communication from outsiders to the community expressed in terms of the indigenous cultural forms that are used. We should also note that the communication does not take place exclusively through words. There are things to see and touch and taste, and there is body movement in terms of various postures and processions. This would suggest that not all meaning in worship is received in terms of rational concepts and mental images.

The multidimensionality of communication and meaning in worship should serve as a warning to those who might be tempted to force worship to go in certain directions. On the practical level, such efforts are unrealistic because they ignore the fact of variation in human temperament and the need for what Jaroslav Pelikan called "liturgical spread." On the theoretical level, worship is too dynamic to be manipulated by behavioralists or systematized by theologians. The liturgy provides us with access to experiences of intimacy and awe, intelligibility and mystery, the natural and the supernatural, history and eschatology, time and eternity, immanence and transcendence, the world and God, the realm of matter and the reality of the Spirit—to name only a few polarities. Liturgical data is so subtle and complex that it ought to give even the boldest theologians pause if they have any notion of trying to explain it.

Furthermore, these polarities are present simultaneously. It is in the earthly assembly ("where two or three are gathered together in my name") that the risen and ascended Lord Jesus is present. The material gifts of bread and wine become the bearers of the body and blood of Christ broken and spilled on Calvary's cross. The directions of communication are also simultaneous. The preacher's sermon may be the word of God addressed to the congregation; but it is also the preacher's own offering to God. A hymn may well be a sacrifice of praise that the congregation renders to God; but it may also preach to the congregation that sings it.

What should be the *order* of worship? In what sequence should things happen? We may think that we need to go through the confessional rite of purification at the beginning of worship. But Isaiah didn't confess his unworthiness until *after* he was granted a vision of the Lord high and lifted up in the Temple. Modern worshipers may be able to experience true contrition only after their defenses have been pierced by the word. We might note the rubric in the *Lutheran Book of Worship* which specifies that prayers of confession may be included in the intercessions if the Brief Order for Confession and Forgiveness has not been used before the service. Similar provision for a prayer of confession and absolution is made in *The Book of Common Prayer*. *The United Methodist Hymnal* locates Confession and Pardon between the intercessions and the greeting of peace. While these new liturgies end in an act of sending forth, a service could also end in a burst of praise.

Who is wise enough to say how or where any one of these elements should be located? Certain patterns of worship have evolved over the course of the centuries, and who are we to say that we can improve on what countless generations of Christians have found meaningful? To be sure, we will make our own contributions to the ever-evolving liturgy of the church; but we can only approach the historic liturgy with a sense of awe for what it represents.

Why, then, would anyone be interested in "creative liturgy?" Probably because such people sincerely view worship primarily as a means of affecting human response or effecting human change rather than as an act of encounter between God and his people. Devotion is calculatingly offered with an eye to the human rather than noncalculatingly to the divine. Worship is seen as directed toward human ends rather than the glorification of God. Such an approach toward worship is the consequence of the *utilitarianism* that pervades our culture and is reflected in so many of our attitudes and activities. The ethos of practical usefulness is one of the chief characteristics of American culture. Since we are inescapably a part of our culture, we bring it to church with us. But it can only result in corrupting worship.

Paul Hoon speaks of *"the corruption of utilitarianism."*[1] On the crude level examples include invitations to come to worship with an appeal to self-interest: "The family that prays together stays together." On a less crude level, it is evident in the propagandizing with which denominational bureaucracies use worship to "promote" various causes and concerns. Thus, the last Sunday in December is designated "Student Recognition Sunday," because it is assumed that college students will be home for Christmas vacation. "Christian family week" ends on the second Sunday in May so that it may coincide with Mother's Day (which sometimes also bumps up against important Sundays in the church-year calendar, such as Pentecost). Holy week itself was preempted in one denomination as a time to hold services and events expressing concern for the situation in Central America. Local congregations also find ways of turning worship into exercizes or programs in evangelism, parish education, social ministry or stewardship.

It has also been discovered that some congregational programs help to hike attendance at worship. Such programs may be Boy Scout Sunday or a special musical presented by the youth choir. Having something for children always brings out adults. This has been the case no less in modern American synagogues than in churches. Rabbi Larry Hoffman writes about "the subtle 'programming' of worship time with speakers, events, music, and happenings that lay to rest the notion that anyone really expects to pray here." He calls this a matter of sending "mixed messages."

> On the one hand we preach the supreme importance of prayer. But when prayer comes into conflict with something else—a recognition of scouting or a display of supposed denominational unity, for example—we do not practice what we preach. And that is the other message. We all know that one is judged by what one does, not by what one says.[2]

The real message we are sending in all this is that the liturgy, the church year, the life of prayer are not all that important: they can be intruded upon for practical reasons such as promoting worthy causes or increasing worship attendance.

Of course, the other side of the truth is that worship must be engaged with life. We do want to draw people into the worship of God. Worship that is unrelated to the realities of vocation, of family life, of Christian responsibilities in society, has ceased to be relevant. There are many people who will come to recognize Boy Scouts or enjoy the singing of the youth choir who are not attuned to "the art of prayer." But the liturgy itself is a more than adequate resource for ministry without having to tailor it toward particular ends. And if some people, who attend special events in connection with worship, are not attuned to the practices of worship, it does not necessarily follow that they find such practices offensive. Some non-church people take vicarious comfort from the fact that there are places where worship is still intact, and that they, too, might have access to it when they need it.

As an example of the suitability of the liturgy to serve as a "resource" for ministry, consider the relationship between worship and evangelism. What is evangelism but the proclamation of the *evangel*, the good news that Jesus' death and resurrection has released the life and values of the new age of the kingdom of God into the old order of decay, sin and death? Our liturgical texts proclaim this with undiminished clarity. They make public statements of the gospel which most of us would not be bold enough to make in a private one-on-one conversation. That, of course, is a function of ritual: to enable us to say and do in public what we would hardly dare to say and do in private. So the liturgy itself is a model for evangelical proclamation that, if followed, would save evangelism from becoming ecclesiastical propagandizing. But this is not the same as using liturgy or worship as an evangelistic tool, which usually means tailoring it to our assumptions of the needs and desires of the unchurched, or developing techniques calculated to produce certain emotional responses.

Liturgy is "the public work of the people of God." It is what the community of faith does in the presence of God and of one another to articulate its own beliefs and values. It should reflect the heritage of the community which performs it so that the witness it makes to outsiders is to say what this community is all about.

Worship is the devotion that the people of God offer to the God who called them into being and made them his own. To affirm this is not to subscribe to the theological cliché that worship should be conducted *soli Deo gloria*—"to the glory of God alone." The God who is the object of Christian worship is never *solus;* the Father of our Lord Jesus Christ is always involved in human history. His *gloria* is always revealed in human life. This is the reality

30

of the incarnation which stands at the center of the Christian revelation. We worship a God who comes to meet us where we are, with all our failures and shortcomings. In a famous sermon entitled, "Epiphany, Glory, and 63rd Street," Joseph Sittler explicated glory as a gift, an evocation, and a demand.[3]

For this reason there is another and opposite corruption of worship that must be addressed. Paul Hoon calls it *"the corruption of aestheticism."*[4] If utilitarianism views worship as a tool to accomplish ends other than the congregation's service to God, aestheticism regards worship as an end in itself. If utilitarianism tailors worship to affect the moral will and elicit certain human responses, aestheticism tailors worship to maximize its sensual pleasure. Consequently, artistic canons are often regarded as decisive for determining the substance and form of worship.

There is an important role for art and for the liturgical artist in worship. But liturgical art is not just religious art in general, or even Christian art in particular. It's not even necessarily the ecclesiastical art advertised in the church publication house catalogues. Liturgical art is diaconal art which serves the word of God. It probes the biblical message in poetry and sound, in textures and colors, in fabrics and glass, in order to give new insight and to provoke response. The liturgical artist is a "deacon" who serves the people of God by enabling them to intensify and remember their words by putting them to musical tones; by crafting altars, fonts, and vessels to serve as earthen vessels for sacramental realities; by designing vestments, paraments, and banners to promote the historical continuity of the church, orient one to sacred times and places, and communicate the gospel by visible words; and by building houses to shelter the assembly, houses which are both home to the church and which point to the heavenly Jerusalem toward which we journey. This means that liturgical art is kerygmatic, sacrificial, and communal. It proclaims the gospel. The artist provides what the people can handle, not just what expresses his or her vision or concept. And it is meant for the use and enjoyment of all—not just for an elite group of aesthetes.

There are, of course, several ways in which liturgy and art deal with the same media. They both employ images and rhetoric that is symbolic. They both understand man as *animal symbolicum*, as Ernst Cassirer put it[5]—as a symbol-making and symbol-using animal. And they both regard physical matter as meaning-bearing, as revelatory. The whole sacramental life of the church is predicated on the proposition that physical elements can be the means of grace by the word of God operating in, with, and through them. To ignore the potentiality of physical matter to convey the spiritual is to violate the very structure of human personality. Humanity cannot be less sensuous in its worship of God than God has been in his creation of the world and the salvation of his human creatures by means of the incarnation of his only-begotten Son. Furthermore, both art and liturgy perform a kind of existential function. At their best they deal with the human situation, the need for people to be saved from illusions about themselves, and to be confronted with the fatefulness of their decisions. That is, both art and liturgy make us vulnerable to the truth about ourselves. They also deal with us ontologically. They address our need "to be" and deal with our ultimate concerns. If we can stretch the term a little, both art and liturgy function eschatologically: they open up dimensions of newness that were not there before, possibilities which we did not see.

Given these affinities, we must insist that to reject the corruption of aestheticism in worship is not to deny the liturgical function of art. Yet there needs to be a theological critique of the role of art in worship. One wonders why worship is always linked with music and the arts in denominational program staffs and in theological seminaries.

Why are commissions on worship not linked with faith and order commissions? Why is the worship professor not as much related to the biblical, historical, and theological departments in our seminaries as he or she is to the practical department? On the other hand, we need artists in our denominational bureaucracies and theological seminaries so that we may also have an artistic critique of art. That might have the effect of halting the production of gaudy stoles and brass appointments, of revolving altars and pre-fab baptismal fonts. All of these media communicate both to church members and non-church members something about who we are and what we are about. We need artists who can prevent us from communicating less about ourselves than we ought to, and who can assist us in saying what we really mean to say. But that does assume the premier role of theology in the life of the church.

Theology, turning its cool reflective gaze on the arts, would conclude that art is not just a neutral way of experiencing reality or expressing vision. With a certain inevitability art becomes a declaration of what is real. Consequently, it has its own vision to impose, its own gospel to proclaim, its own devotees to cultivate. The nature of ultimate reality reported by art is not to be equated with reality as revealed in Jesus Christ. Christians should not be fooled by the fact that the artist may use biblical or liturgical texts and images. I have heard a number of performances in churches of Brahms' *German Requiem.* Brahms used biblical texts—edited—instead of the traditional liturgical texts of the requiem mass. His work is, to my taste, one of the finest choral pieces in the nineteenth-century literature, and I would go even to churches to hear it performed well. To hear it may be for me a satisfying aesthetic experience, or even a religious experience; but it is not an act of Christian worship. The name of Jesus doesn't appear once in the work. But the mention of Jesus' name is no guarantee that the work is liturgically suitable.

What makes a work liturgically suitable is that it can be an expression of the "public work of the people of God," or at least by a portion of them who form that part of the congregation known as the choir. And what the choir sings should be proportionate to the liturgy as a whole. A ten-minute alleluia verse is simply too much to serve the purpose of covering a gospel procession in most church buildings.

But there's an element of truth that needs to be considered here, too. A conversation between T. S. Eliot and the German poet M. Hausmann illustrates the concern I am raising. Hausmann voiced misgivings about Bach's *St. Matthew Passion* as a liturgical form. Used in this way, he contended, Bach's music is like being pleasantly told that one's brother has been killed in a concentration camp under terrible circumstances.

> And now comes a friend and tells you of your brother's agony in an aria with orchestral accompaniment. What would you say to that? Could you really take the man seriously? Would not everything in you revolt . . . ? But if the aria was so wonderful and the music so glorious that you forgot the horror of the crime, if the art so hid reality that it almost ceases to be true, what kind of role of deceit would art be playing then? And this is exactly what Bach did in the *St. Matthew Passion.* Just look at the people who attend. . . . Are they listening to an account of the Passion? Not at all; they are listening to art. Bach certainly did not intend this but he brought it about.[6]

It should be pointed out that Bach was aware of this peril. Jaroslav Pelikan points out that Bach's greatness as a church composer lay precisely in the consecration of his artistic talent to the service of the gospel.[7] The church music of Bach, both choral and instrumental, can be profitably studied for its theological as well as its aesthetic sensitivities. For that very reason it is with great reluctance that I must conclude that Hausmann has a point. The reality of Good Friday—of the only-begotten Son of God going to the limit of death and God-forsakenness to accomplish our redemption—is so stark that the church has for centuries not celebrated the eucharist on this day (Lutheran practice notwithstanding) and has preferred no instruments used in worship other than the naked human voice.

Which leads me to say that sometimes liturgy will prefer ugliness to beauty as a more truthful way of expressing the divine-human encounter which occurs in the act of worship. Let us remember that the Holy is *tremendum* as well as *fascinans;* that it repels as well as attracts. Worship whose forms offend may more authentically enable humans to meet God than worship which only gives pleasure. The historian of religion, Gerhard van der Leeuw, points out that

> the least "beautiful" images of the gods are wont to be the most holy. . . . A good part of them are fetishes. . . . Primitive man finds . . . the distance which separates him from the wholly other to be better expressed by the non-human or the semihuman. From the religious point of view, the Greeks ranked the xoanon, an ancient image of the god made of wood, rough and scarcely human, above the works of a Phildias or a Praxiteles. . . . The Roman Catholic knows that the most holy images of Christ, the Blessed Virgin, or other saints, blackened with age, are only rarely the most important works of art. . . . Thus it is possible for faith to prefer the ugly to the beautiful, because . . . [the ugly] better preserves the distance which separates the holy.[8]

Worship which is in Spirit—the Holy Spirit—and in truth—the truth of the gospel and the truth about where we are in relation to God and to one another—may prefer the simple to the complex, the ugly to the beautiful. Humble parishes may have neither the resources nor the talent to be great cathedrals. Church musicians may have to work with a choir of six amateurs in terms of what is possible and satisfying for them, and may have to conclude (after some patient efforts) that the congregation cannot grasp the rhythms and intervals of sixteenth and seventeenth century chorales. The congregation is not there to serve the music; the music is to be placed in the service of the public work of this particular assembly of God's people. We need our most creative church musicians, as well as our most competent pastors, in small congregations where creativity and ingenuity are daily job requirements. This argues for a church structure which makes it possible for talented leaders to work in what are usually low-salary situations: in other words, a collegial or diocesan polity rather than a congregationalist one.

It also needs to be asked, by any worship leader in any congregation, what it means to worship in an age of holocaust. If our worship is to have integrity, if it is to be done in Spirit and in truth, we need to be able to articulate before God our own experience of this world and of human history, our own sense of the presence and the absence of God in our times. As the Roman Catholic theologian, David Power, has asked, "Can we in truth celebrate eucharist after the Nazi holocaust and in the face of an imminent nuclear holocaust, and in a world half-populated by refugees, in the same way as we did before the occurrence of such horrors?"[9] Is worship truly spiritual and spiritually true which is silent about all this and which does not somehow express the experience of God's absence as well as his presence?

There has been a tendency recently to make worship an "upbeat" experience. Lost sometimes in the happy atmosphere of services styled to make people "feel good" about themselves and about God has been a sense of *con-*

trition or sorrow for personal and corporate culpabilities, and *lament* over the human situation. Yet expressions of contrition and lament pervade the liturgy—not only in the Confession of Sins but also in the midst of songs of praise. No sooner do we sing "Glory to God in the highest" than we interject the petition, "Lord God, Lamb of God, you take away the sin of the world: have mercy on us." Many of the psalms are categorized by form critics as psalms of lament, and these are included in the responsorial psalm after the first lesson and in the psalmody of the daily prayer offices. It is noteworthy that many of these psalms of lament end on a note of praise. For example, Psalm 22, which begins, "My God, my God, why have you forsaken me? and are so far from my cry, and from the words of my distress?" ends with words of praise and hope, so as to suggest that the community's constant praise of God is able to accommodate individual lament. On the other hand, there are also shifts from thanksgiving to lament, as in Nehemiah 9, which is in many ways the mother of all praying in the synagogue and in the church. God's people give thanks to him with great confidence, and in the act of *thanksgiving* proclaim God's mighty acts. Then we shift to *supplication* and *intercession* so as to beseech God to bring to fruition what he has begun, and to fulfillment what he has promised. It is right that contemporary liturgical revision has found a prominent place for intercession in the eucharistic liturgy and in the prayer offices. Intercession is a plea for the triumph of God's purposes in spite of all appearances to the contrary, and it suitably expresses the sense of God's absence.

The sense of absence implies a relationship, as Geoffrey Wainwright points out: "It presupposes what has been, or it anticipates what might become, a divine presence 'for us;' it remembers a taste or betokens a desire not yet satisfied. The no-longer or not-yet of God's saving presence is a sign that the transcendent God remains his own,

37

to give or to withhold himself."[10] Why would God with-hold himself? It may be, as Dietrich Bonhoeffer sug-gested,[11] that God is teaching us to get along without him so that when we come to him it will not be to use him as a "working hypothesis" but so that we can freely enter into the personal communion which the God and Father of our Lord Jesus Christ desires us to enjoy. Others may just find themselves sharing that same sense of God's forsakenness expressed in Jesus' cry on the cross, "My God, my God, why hast thou forsaken me?" Evangelical proclamation will plant the cross of Christ in all human depths. But let us also note that the cross was the supreme moment of free human surrender to God. So there, too, God was present in the depths, giving himself in love to reestablish commu-nion between himself and his fallen human creatures.

Most of us have experienced the sense of God's ab-sence. The public liturgy of the church is no stranger to the paradox of God's absence and presence, because it is cele-brated only and precisely where we are: living between the already and the not-yet of salvation, between our call to the new life of the world to come and this same old world of sin and death. The church has a sense of itself as the eschatology community, heralding and modeling the new order of the kingdom of God; but it is not itself the king-dom, and therefore it lives and moves and has its being in the midst of the old order. It knows the presence of God in Christ through his Spirit along the way of history, in the preaching of the gospel and the administration of the sacra-ments. This communal assurance of God's presence will offer support to the individual member who may be more acutely aware, in private experience, of God's apparent ab-sence and his own lack of a sense of relatedness to God. But that is one of the roles the liturgy plays: it helps to form the faith of the faithful and offers spiritual support during times of distress and unbelief. This argues above all that it should be there when it is needed. And that argues against undue tampering with it other than following the options, customs, and special rites of the church year. Respect for the tradition is not in the interest of antiquarianism; it is in the interest of pastoral care, as Luther so rightly understood when he explained that he had been hesitant to get into the work of liturgical revision "partly because of the weak in faith, who cannot suddenly exchange an old and accustomed order of worship for a new and unusual one, and more so because of the fickle and fastidious spirits who rush in like unclean swine without faith or reason, and who delight only in novelty and tire of it as quickly, when it has worn off. Such people are a nuisance even in other affairs, but in spiritual matters, they are absolutely unbearable."[12]

Nevertheless, Luther went on to admit, "we must dare something in the name of Christ." We, too, have just gone through a period of radical liturgical change. The dust must have a chance to settle and people have to have an opportunity to grow into the new or renewed rites, led by pastors who will respect the integrity of the rites, as spelled out in the rubrics, while wrestling with the integrity of worship in Spirit and in truth. The theologically well-educated and the spiritually well-intentioned seem to think that the mark of good communication is never having to repeat something. Yet, as poets, composers, and artists know, rhythm makes things memorable; and as good teachers know, repetition constantly reasserts. Liturgical repetition and rhythm are to be fostered, and change should reflect the considered consensus of the whole community of faith—not pastoral whim. Otherwise there is no meaningful way to speak of liturgy as "the public work of the whole people of God."

39

The Mission of the Church: Defective Concepts of Evangelism

Why does the church gather for worship? Why does it reach out to others in acts of witness? It is because the church has a place in the mission of God. God created humankind to be in communion with himself. In that act of human disregard of God which theology calls "the Fall," communion was broken. The history of salvation can be defined as the attempt of God to restore communion with fallen and estranged humanity.

God did this by choosing one people out of all the peoples of the earth to be "my own possession," "a kingdom of priests and a holy nation" (Ex 19:6). By its holiness, i.e., its sense of belonging to God, this people—Israel—will attract other people to the service of God. This vocation is most clearly articulated in the Second and Third Isaiah: "I will give you as a light to the nations, that my salvation may reach to the end of the earth" (Isa 49:6). "Arise, shine; for your light has come, and the glory of the Lord has risen upon you. For behold, darkness shall cover the earth, and thick darkness the peoples; but the Lord will arise upon you, and his glory will be seen upon you. And nations shall come to your light, and kings to the brightness of your rising" (Isa 60:1–3).

The nations, the Gentiles, coming to the knowledge and worship of the God of Israel were increasingly seen as a sign of the end-time, the *eschaton*, when Israel's vocation would be fulfilled. In the words of Isaiah, Israel is to rise from the hopelessness of its situation, because the epiphany or manifestation of Yahweh will fill Zion with light. With the rest of the world covered in darkness, Zion's magnetic force will pull the nations toward her. The Jews of the dispersion will arrive with these Gentiles (Isa 60:4a literally reads: "your sons they bring them from afar"). Other offerings by land and sea are the wealth and possessions of the nations (vv 5–7). This great vision of the salvation of God for all, along with Psalm 72, furnishes much of the language for Matthew's story of the visit of the magi and even more for the legendary expansion of the story (i.e., the three kings). Indeed, the coming of the Gentiles to pay homage to the messiah of the Jews can be understood as a proleptic fulfillment of eschatological hopes.

In the "fullness of time" God sent his Son, who served God's mission of reconciling all humanity to himself by being obedient even unto death on the cross. In the act of resurrection God vindicated the meaning and message of Jesus. The book of Acts is full of this kind of proclamation (*kerygma*) by the apostles of Jesus who were "witnesses" of the risen Lord, and were empowered by his Spirit to be his *apostoloi* ("sent ones"). The apostles turned Israel's vocation to attract the nations into mission: they go to the nations under the authority of Christ himself: "All authority in heaven and on earth has been given to me. Go therefore and make disciples of all nations, baptizing them in the name of the Father and of the Son and of the Holy Spirit, teaching them to observe all that I have commanded you; and lo, I am with you always, to the close of the age" (Mt 28:18–20).

The first sentence of this "great commission" is almost a verbatim quotation of Daniel 7:14: "Authority was

41

given unto him." In Daniel this investment with authority is consequent upon the coming to the Ancient of Days of the Son of man whom all nations are to serve. In Matthew this investment has evidently taken place through the ascension of the One whose command is to make disciples of all nations. Since the consequence of the exaltation of the Son of man is that all nations are to serve him, the mission of the disciples of Jesus is to proclaim that the exaltation of the messiah has already taken place. Christ's lordship over heaven and earth has begun: the church's task is to proclaim Christ's lordship as gospel. The apostolic task is not just to win converts; it is to proclaim what has already happened and to invite those who hear the announcement to join in the worship and service of this messiah.

It was, of course, an audacious thing for a small, persecuted minority within the Roman superstate to proclaim the lordship of Jesus Christ. But such an act of proclamation (kerygma) is known in our own historical experience. When President Abraham Lincoln issued the Emancipation Proclamation in 1863, it was based on his war powers authority as president, and therefore could only apply to the rebel states, which were still largely in control of rebel forces. Nor, in spite of the defeat of General Lee's army at Gettysburg, was the liberation of these states a foregone conclusion. Nevertheless, the proclamation of freedom was made and an offer of pardon and amnesty was extended to all southerners who would take an oath of allegiance to the Union and all the wartime policies concerning slavery and emancipation. The proclamation was good news to slaves but was also directed toward final (may we say, eschatological?) fulfillment. In this sense it was not unlike the mission authorized by Jesus in Luke 24 to proclaim repentance and forgiveness of sins "to all nations, beginning from Jerusalem."

As the "spirit of freedom" embodied in the abolitionist movement stood behind the Emancipation Proclamation, so the "Spirit of Jesus Christ" embodied in the church energized Christ's mission. There is a pneumatological as well as a christological basis for mission. Paul is emphatic that the mission of the Spirit is the consequence of and in succession to the mission of the Son. "But when the time had fully come, God sent forth his Son, born of woman, born under the law, to redeem those who were under the law, so that we might receive adoption as sons. And because you are sons, God has sent the Spirit of his Son into our hearts, crying 'Abba! Father' " (Gal 4:4–6). In Paul's view the adopted son had the full rights of sonship (which would have been the Greco-Roman custom); such an adopted child is not just halfway into the household, as the Judaizers suggested. This is because the adopted children receive the Spirit of the Son. The use of the phrase "Spirit of the Son," rather than "Spirit of God," is not casual. The Spirit inspires to speak, and the first word of the adopted child is *Abba* (for which Paul uses the Aramaic). This is the "spirit of sonship."

The Spirit is the promise of the Father whom Christ sends forth. Hence the Johannine form of the commission is immediately followed by the statement of the risen Lord, "he breathed on them, and said to them, 'Receive the Holy Spirit' " (Jn 20:22–23). The promise of the power of the Spirit is closely related to mission in the first chapter of Acts. ". . . you shall receive power when the Holy Spirit has come upon you; and you shall be my witnesses in Jerusalem and in all Judea and Samaria and to the end of the earth" (Acts 1:8). The coming of the Spirit on the day of Pentecost, the "the great and manifest day" prophesied by Joel, is the beginning of this mission of witnessing under the guidance of the Holy Spirit. There is no need to demonstrate this by going through Acts chapter by chapter. It is sufficient to repeat and endorse the findings of Roland Allen, after he made such a survey: "The conclusion is inevi-

43

table, that the Spirit given was, in St. Luke's view, a Spirit which impelled to missionary work, in fact a missionary Spirit."[1] Hence, there is an inseparable connection between the Holy Spirit and our participation in the mission of God authorized by Christ.

Once we can appreciate both the christological and the pneumatological bases of mission, we are in a position to realize more fully the extent to which mission is brought into being and put into effect by God himself. The triune God is the source of the missionary enterprise in which the church is invited to participate. What does such participation mean? It means, in the first place, that the church is to reproduce the pattern of the incarnation of Christ. The Christian life is the life of Christ lived in his disciples, under the power and guidance of the Holy Spirit. What does this mean? As Dietrich Bonhoeffer wrote: "In the incarnation God makes himself known as him who wishes to exist not for himself but 'for us.' Consequently, in view of the incarnation of God, to live as man before God can mean only to exist not for oneself but for God and for other men."[2] So the only conceivable form of the church is that of a servant. Inseparable from service is the path of suffering. Paul declared that he rejoiced in his sufferings and completed "what is lacking in Christ's afflictions" (Col 1:24). In other words, Paul's sufferings were signs of the continuation of the messianic vocation and mission in the world. Here is where we link up with the New Testament understanding of witness as *martyria.*

It is important to stress that this suffering service, this *diakonia,* is not the means of accomplishing the mission. God will not establish his kingdom through our acts of service. But our acts of service will bear witness to the present reality of God's kingdom. In other words, we are not to heal the sick in order to convert them; we are to heal because this is a sign of the overflowing of God's love for humanity, and his will for the wholeness of his creation. By its activities and by its very life the church witnesses to the love of God. It never points to itself. It has to say, with the Christ of the fourth gospel, "if I bear witness of myself, my witness is not true" (Jn 5:31). Jesus points to the words and deeds of his Father; we point to the words and deeds of the Christ.

If it can be accepted that our witness is a participation in the mission of God, then there are certain concepts of mission or evangelism which must be regarded as defective. Examination of these concepts to see in what ways they are misconceptions, and therefore misleading, will help to clarify the meaning of witness we are pursuing. Among several possible defective concepts, I want to concentrate on two: (1) the idea that evangelism is primarily concerned with individual salvation; and (2) the idea that evangelism is church extension and proselytism.

The understanding of evangelism in terms of the salvation or rescue of individuals stems originally from Pietism and has been characteristic of the revivalist movements. In all fairness, we must admit that the early Pietist leaders, such as Jacob Philip Spener and Nicholas von Zinzendorf, could only envision personal spiritual awakening within the support structures of a community also undergoing spiritual renewal. And the Second Great Awakening in early nineteenth-century America aligned revivalism with some of the most important social causes of the day, such as abolition of slavery and temperance. Nevertheless, by the late nineteenth century revivalism seemed only concerned with salvation of the soul, to the neglect of the saved person's social responsibilities. It conveyed the idea that the saved person is to be removed from the world of daily life and relocated into some kind of religious enclave. To be sure, one may have to earn a living in the world, but this was seen as irrelevant to one's main concern—

salvation. But, as D. T. Niles has said: "The end-event of Christian life is not simply salvation of the person but a new heaven and a new earth."[3]

The kind of evangelism which calls one into a spiritual life regards secular existence as irrelevant, except insofar as it provides a sphere for the exercise of piety and patience. The convert may have been rescued, but the gospel has not been preached to the world. This dichotomy between the spiritual and the material is contrary to the biblical outlook. Responding to the German materialist philosopher Friedrich Feuerbach's assertion that "man is what he eats," the Orthodox theologian Alexander Schmemann argued, in his classic book *For the Life of the World*, that man is indeed what he eats.

> . . . the Bible . . . also begins with man as a hungry being, with the man who is that which he eats. The perspective, however, is wholly different, for nowhere in the Bible do we find the dichotomies which for us are the self-evident framework of all approaches to religion. In the Bible the food man eats, the world of which he must partake in order to live, is given to him by God, and it is given as *communion with God*. The world as man's food is not something "material" and limited to material functions, thus different from, and opposed to, the specifically "spiritual" functions by which man is related to God. All that exists is God's gift to man, and it all exists to make God known to man, to make man's life communion with God. It is divine love made food, made life for man. God *blesses* everything He creates, and, in biblical language, this means that He makes all creation the sign and means of His presence and wisdom, love and revelation: "O taste and see that the Lord is good."[4]

The pietistic and revivalist interpretation of evangelism is further wrong, in the words of Walter Freytag, "in not taking seriously the fact that the Lord Christ is already Lord of the world, and that the Kingdom of God exists in righteousness, peace and joy, in which we serve. That is more than a condition of the soul; it is the Lordship of Christ brought to reality in the world."[5] Thus, the emphasis on conversion, understood in terms of individual salvation, means that private experience replaces public responsibility. As Gibson Winter wrote, this stress on individual salvation is "a pietistic diversion of energies and resources which only confuses Christians and non-Christians as to the message of the Gospel, the nature of the Church and the task of Christianity"[6] in the world, for it results in the belief that the preaching of an individualistic gospel will produce the reconciliation of society. Hence, the church's task is understood to consist in the spreading of the gospel while social problems are taken care of by others, who may only incidentally be members of churches. According to Gibson Winter,

> The only answer to this pietistic tradition is that the Gospel embraces the whole of human life and society. Man's life in society is an interdependent web. Personal immortality is no more nor less accessible to spiritual renewal than racial discrimination in housing. A narrow spirituality refuses to recognize the interdependence and wholeness of life; its concern rejects involvement, and its preoccupation with individual piety derives from the false assumption that the individual soul is more open to change than social institutions.[7]

The understanding of evangelism as individual salvation continues to appeal to many church people because the church is still largely based on residential communities. Individual conversion corresponds to the areas of private concern—family, home, children, local schools, local politics, etc. These are all legitimate concerns of the church, but they do not constitute the whole of the church's mission and they can indeed divert Christians from a wider vision of their task.

The church exists "for the life of the world" (kosmos), and the world is larger than the domestic settings of the church's members. The church as a whole has steadily retreated from larger spheres of reality over the course of the last several centuries in the wake of advances in human knowledge and new political arrangements. This created a vacuum into which other understandings and visions of reality poured their claims. These competing visions of reality also insinuated their claims into the households which the church is concerned to Christianize. If the church is to present a coherent view of reality, it cannot avoid confrontation and dialogue with other views of reality, especially those offered by claimants to totalitarian control over our lives such as business, science, and the modern state.

It makes no sense to be engaged in mission without considering the opposition. Business is no longer just the transfer of wealth in exchange for goods or services; it is also a series of abstract economic "forces" regulated by political ideologies which are given governmental shape in this or that policy. Science is no longer just the knowledge achieved by the use of ostensibly objective methods; it is also the provider of technologies that purport to make our lives better through chemistry. The modern state is no longer just the executive function of deliberating people or their representatives; it is also the bureaucracy which survives changes in administration and coerces the people with economic indicators, tax policies, behavioral modification techniques such as quota systems or threats of institutionalization such as dissenters in the former Soviet Union were routinely subjected to and frequently experienced. This is "the world," which in St. John's gospel is ambiguously the object of God's saving concern and also the arena of the evil one from which the "elect" must be rescued. Dealing with the world requires all the intelligence and knowledge the church can muster, and at least a willingness to project a counter vision of reality through solid preaching and teaching.

A purely pietistic approach to mission leads to an escape from public responsibility into areas of private concern. The concentration of the church on domestic life means that whole areas of modern life lie outside of the bounds of the church's witness, and are not affected by it. But Christ came "that they may have life" (Jn 10:10). This life is the superabundant life of God, the life of the world to come, life in accordance with the divine will. It therefore demands a response from the human creature in his total being. This "life" is not restricted to religious concerns, but includes all aspects of culture, all activities in every corner of society.

Not only does the pietistic interpretation of evangelism falsify the true task of Christianity to address the gospel to the whole world, it also rests on a misunderstanding of the corporate nature of the church, because, as Winter suggests, "it isolates individual decision from the total content of the proclamation and pure teaching in which it receives its authentic grounding and continuity."[8] His perceptive comments are worth quoting further. He argues that this approach reduces Christianity to subjective feelings and limits it to the experience of a personal relationship with Christ.

> All the rest flows from this: the authenticity of the preaching is not tested by tradition or apostolic symbol but by its power to evoke such personal decisions; the validity of the Church's life does not rest upon its unity, holiness, apostolicity but upon the presence in its midst of those who have made decisions and had experiences; the task of the churches in society is not

49

> defined with reference to the redemption of creation amidst the ambiguities of sin, for the health of society is an inevitable effect flowing from the presence of "converted" individuals.[9]

This however does not exhaust the *gravamina* against this concept of evangelism. Its over-subjectivity has to be further stressed. It reduces the *kerygma*, which is the proclamation of certain facts, of what God has done and is doing, to a recital of personal experiences calculated to reproduce the same experiences in the hearers. The church's witness becomes individual testimony to what God has done *for me*, whereas the true apostolic witness is to what God has done in Christ for the life of the world. A. R. Vidler's strictures are indeed valid:

> The revivalist movements, which have been, and are likely to remain, periodically recurring events in the history of Christianity, tend to bring the idea of conversion into discredit among wise and balanced minds by their aggressive insistence that all real Christians, as they would say, must undergo a psychological experience of change, sudden in its incidence and uniform in its pattern. That the managers of revivalist movements should like to work according to a uniform and therefore easily manageable technique is intelligible but it is gravely deplorable. For the attempt to dragoon souls into conformity with a single, and in fact none too healthy, pattern of spiritual experience disregards the diverse means by which the Spirit of God actually works.[10]

Vidler wrote these words in 1938, but in the recurring revivalistic movements we continue to see a stress on *"the way,"* aligned with a certain number of fundamental principles, and predictable attempts to manipulate human experience along well-trodden paths. Maybe human needs

50

are much the same in all ages, but the basic existential questions differ. In the words of Paul Tillich, humanity

> experiences his present situation in terms of disruption, conflict, self-destruction, meaninglessness, and despair in all realms of life. . . . The question arising out of this experience is not, as in the Reformation, the question of a merciful God and the forgiveness of sins; nor is it, as in the early Greek Church, the question of finitude, of death and error; nor is it the question of the personal religious life, or of the Christianization of culture and society. It is the question of a reality in which the self-estrangement of our existence is overcome, a reality of reconciliation and reunion, of creativity, meaning and hope.[11]

We need to come to terms with the basic issues raised by life in our time, the kind of questions prompted by the ambiguities of our own historical, social, cultural, and economic experiences. The recognition that we need to address the real human predicament with the gospel and not an imagined one means that we must listen and learn before we try to speak and teach. As J. V. Taylor has suggested:

> The evangelism that proceeds by listening and learning, entering into another man's vision in order to see Christ in it, does not start with assertions about sin but waits to be told about it. And usually the truth about sin is almost the last truth to be told.[12]

Unless this is accepted, there is a danger that the call to salvation from sin will exacerbate the condition of those to whom we relate the gospel. "A Christ who releases me from guilt that has been induced, and forgives sins of which the Church but not my conscience has accused me, will not be the Saviour of my world."[13]

51

The study of conversion has been greatly accelerated by examination of the so-called "brainwashing" done by a variety of cults and radical sects among American youth in the 1960s and 1970s.[14] Some have isolated certain psychological, sociological, and accidental factors that can be used to actually "predict" a conversion. Some have regarded conversion as an emotional crisis, and others have seen it more cognitively as a decision-making process. None of these studies should suggest that evangelism should not have conversion as its goal. There is no doubt that similarities as well as differences can be seen in the most celebrated instances of conversion in Christian history, such as those of Paul, Augustine, Martin Luther, and John Wesley. In each case a crisis long in brewing bubbled over, triggered by something external to themselves: Paul blinded after seeing a light and falling from his horse; Augustine hearing the singing of a child; Luther receiving a sudden flash of insight while sitting in his privy; Wesley feeling his heart "strangely warmed." Aidan Kavanagh notes that "In these and many other accounts one notices an imperceptibly growing realization that the normalcy of life lived within the conventions of one's own world is but the face of death itself."[15] These experiences of transformation turn one away from the normalcy of life rather than plugging one into it.

The catechumenate of the ancient church was designed to facilitate conversion by fostering that sense of repentance or *metanoia* that would orient one in a new direction—away from the life of "this world" and toward the life of the world to come lived proleptically. In other words, the catechumenate served the purpose of initiating one into the eschatological community which participates in the mission of God. There was a certain rigor in the catechumenate as described by Hippolytus of Rome in *The Apostolic Tradition* (ca. 215). Candidates for baptism had to give up certain occupations and professions, such as being pimps, prostitutes, gladiators, or even artisans who made idols. On the other hand, they were made to do things they might not otherwise have done, such as honor the widows and visit the sick.[16] The life-style of individual Christians and the church as a whole was to be a witness to the new reality of the kingdom of God, lived in the midst of the old order of sin and death. The seriousness with which this was taken is evident in the structures of public penance in the ancient church, by which those who committed grave sins (murder, adultery, and apostacy) were given a second chance to learn *metanoia* in the order of penitents. Such sins had compromised the integrity of the church's witness and subjected the sanctifying work of the Holy Spirit to a credibility gap. So such sinners were excommunicated, prayed for, engaged in works of discipline and mercy, and finally reconciled with the eucharistic fellowship on Maundy Thursday. Lest we think this is too rigorous, it should be noted that the real rigorists in the ancient church were those who held that the church had no authority to give any second absolution after baptism, although it could pray that God would leave the door of his mercy slightly ajar.

There's no doubt that the catechumenal and penitential processes served the purpose of keeping the church relatively pure and unstained during the age of persecution. Nevertheless, these structures survived and flourished also during the fourth and fifth centuries when many people joined the church, because being a Christian was thought to be advantageous to their careers. Perhaps in such a situation the catechumenate served an even more important purpose of impressing on the candidates for baptism what it was they were really aligning themselves with. It is interesting to note the element of realism that crept into the preaching and teaching of the bishops who had the task of forming the candidates and the newly baptized into the Christian life-style. For example, on the Sun-

53

day after Easter the newly baptized would remove their white baptismal garments and take their places in the congregation of the faithful. Augustine of Hippo found this to be a welcome occasion to remind his congregation of the significance of Sunday as the "eighth day," the day of resurrection in which Christians enter into a celebration that transcends the limitations of time and space by anticipating the *eschaton*, the end-time. He then enjoins the newly baptized to be watchful, lest in putting off their baptismal garments they should permit the slower process to start which is putting off the Christ-like person, whom they have just put on. "Tomorrow," he then says, "the legal holiday comes to an end and the courts will again be in session, but is that any reason for starting to litigate again, and for tearing each other to pieces?"[17] What Augustine is suggesting in this sermon is that incorporation into the eschatological reality of the new life in Christ has some consequences for how Christians live their lives in society.

This model of conversion and repentance holds up the Christian's responsibility to participate in the mission of God for the transformation of the world by the witness of their lives. Christians are called by baptism into the new reality of the kingdom of God inaugurated in the death and resurrection of Jesus Christ. This has implications for how they live their lives in this world; it also has implications for the life of the world. The model of individual salvation from Pietism and revivalism does not operate from such an eschatological perspective. So instead of the church turning outward to the whole creation, and especially to human society, it turns inward and spends much of its time and energy on the nurture of its members.

There are aspects of the understanding of evangelism as individual salvation which have been held by Lutherans coming from a pietistic heritage or who are influenced by neo-evangelical groups in America. But since the nineteenth century the most common understanding of evangelism among Lutherans has been that of *church exten-sion*. This concept is more ambiguous to treat because a part of God's mission in the world is to have a people who shall be his own, "live under him in his kingdom, and serve him in everlasting righteousness, innocence, and blessed-ness" (Luther). So one would think that the community of the new covenant should extend itself by embracing more and more people in its life and mission, its worship and witness. The problem with the concept of evangelism as church extension is *denominationalism.* Unless we accept the postulate that there is only one true and undivided church and that all heresy and schism is outside of it, we are faced with the problem of defining what church exten-sion means. To speak of church extension today can only mean the extension of the Lutheran Church, or the Roman Catholic Church, or the Baptist Church. Unless we are blind to the existing state of denominationalism, evange-lism as church extension can only mean perpetuating our divisions. We can only extend and plant denominations, each with its own confession, discipline, liturgy, pol-ity, etc.

Those who live comfortably with the concept of evan-gelism as church extension can only be equating the church with the kingdom of God. It is true that those who stress the "not yet" of the kingdom's reality tend to undervalue the church as the first-fruits of the kingdom. But to define evangelism as church extension is, in Freytag's words, "an ecclesiological narrowing of the concept of the Kingdom of God. . . . Christendom is never the Kingdom of God, for all our churches are only provisional in character. They are never the ultimate goal."[18] The church's task is to pro-claim and demonstrate the signs of the kingdom; but it is not to equate itself with the kingdom.

Mission does not begin with the church; it originates in the redemptive purpose of the triune God. The church is included in God's missionary plan; but establishing the church is not the goal of God's plan, it is a means to the end. The reconciliation of all humanity to God and to one another is the goal of God's mission, and a church which is not engaged in this task and does not reflect reconciliation in its own life is not participating in the mission of God. Without this perspective the church misconceives its task, which becomes, not evangelism, but solving internal problems. In the words of James A. Scherer,

> Church-centeredness usually means that (1) mission is abandoned or greatly reduced, in favor of institutional consolidation and ministry to Christians (that is, the Church serves itself, rather than the world); or, (2) mission becomes propaganda for a denomination, and takes the form of spreading denominational institutions and policies.[19]

The basic problem with the concept of evangelism as church extension is that the evangelizing group becomes a substitute for the message it has to proclaim. As a result, our concern is to incorporate new members into our own community with its particular cultural and doctrinal luggage rather than into the eschatological community formed to herald and celebrate the kingdom of God. Yet where can this community exist except in our denominational manifestations of "church"? And how can these churches exist without the cultural and doctrinal luggage which gives them historical identity? It would seem that the most effective witness the church can make to its identification with the eschatological community called, gathered, enlightened, and sanctified by the Holy Spirit is to be "catholic" in its expressions—i.e., to represent the whole of Christian cultural and doctrinal experience and to invite people into a cross-cultural community. The historic Christian liturgy is itself a cross-cultural product, retaining traces of Semitic, Hellenistic, Roman, Gallican, Teutonic, and American forms of expression and expanding now into African and Asian cultures. The historic liturgy is itself a witness to God's plan for the reconciliation of all peoples with himself. Those churches which use the historical liturgical forms are challenged by those forms to reflect the catholicity of their liturgy in the whole of their church life, especially in their membership composition. This means welcoming into membership all who are within reach, regardless of their social, racial, or economic background.

Concern about membership raises one of the most serious problems with the concept of evangelism as church extension, now commonly called "church growth." The tactic often used is *proselytism*. This is the attempt to win over members of another denomination or congregation. Examples of this are legion in American society. We are used to doorbell-ringing missionaries from the Mormons, Jehovah's Witnesses, and Seventh-Day Adventists who try to win over, with their well-rehearsed speeches, even those who express contentment with their faith and their church home. But there are histories of one denomination or congregation trying to recruit members from other denominations or congregations. This has sometimes been done in subtle ways. For example, Methodists in the nineteenth century set up confirmation classes and this just happened to appeal to Scandinavian immigrants of Lutheran background who were perplexed by the welter of churches in the new land, but knew they should look for a church with a confirmation program. Lutherans are now retaliating by trying to "include" minorities in our church life in order to accomplish ideologically-mandated goals to "include" people of color or who use a language other than English, which specifically does not mean dark-haired Norwegians. Where would such people come from except, to a large extent, from traditionally African-American churches, or churches with large Hispanic memberships, which means specifically the Roman Catholic Church? In fact, Roman Catholics have been fair game all along for Protestant churches. Indoctrination once made Catholics impervious to Protestant influences. But large numbers of divorced Catholics have found their way to Protestant ministers and into Protestant congregations as a result of their desire to remarry within a Christian setting. Alienated Catholics have been drawn in droves to the new Yuppie-oriented mega-churches. The 15,000-member Willow Creek Community Church in Barrington, Illinois, reports that more than 50 percent of its members are former Catholics. Willow Creek leaders disclaim that they are raiding the Catholic Church for members; they merely target the unchurched. But a 1985 Gallop Poll found that 24 percent of American Catholics, some 16.5 million people, did not attend services regularly, which makes them fair game for all those churches which are targeting the unchurched. We need to be clear that proselytism is not an acceptable form of evangelism.

The problem with proselytism for Christians is that Jesus condemned it categorically: "Woe to you, scribes and Pharisees, hypocrites! for you traverse sea and land to make a single proselyte, and when he becomes a proselyte, you make him twice as much a child of hell as yourselves" (Mt 23:15). In view of this condemnation by the Lord of the church, we need to know what proselytism is and why it is to be rejected.

Jewish proselytism arose when Israel replaced the rest of the world as the center of Jewish concern. It rests on the conviction of the unique status of the chosen people. Outside of this community there could be no hope. So there were those who believed that the Gentiles could be saved only by embracing the faith and practices of Judaism, or of that party within Judaism to which the proselytizer belonged. Thus, proselytism became a kind of denominational imperialism.

58

Proselytism has characterized Christianity in its historical course even more than Judaism. As long as Christianity was divided along dogmatic, liturgical, or cultural lines, members of one party were always trying to "convert" members of another party. Unlike much of the proselytism that takes place among Christian denominations and congregations today, this older proselytism rested on the conviction that the proselytizing group had a handle on truth. But much proselytizing that has taken place among mainline Christian groups in recent years has been motivated by a scramble for additional members rather than a passion for truth.

The younger churches of Asia and Africa have taken the lead in rejecting the proselytizing approach, and a consequence of this has been ecumenical cooperation in the missionary enterprise, at least among the mainline churches. This can serve as a model for the older Christian churches of Europe and North America. For example, if Lutherans and Anglicans can engage in common missionary work in East Africa, they should be able to do it in North America.

Christians are not called to set one denomination over against another. They are called to set the kingdom of God over against human need. We are to make claims for God and his will, not advance claims for particular religious practices, theological systems, or biblical interpretations. Evangelism is announcing good news, not recruiting church members. As far as new members are concerned, if the unchurched (non-Christians or lapsed Christians) see some correlation between our belief and our behavior, they may very well be attracted to the gospel we preach and desire to join the community which proclaims and celebrates this gospel. If they don't, we still worship the God and Father of our Lord Jesus Christ and witness to his mighty acts, both in the liturgical assembly and in the daily affairs of life in society. As the great missiologist, J. C.

Hoekendijk, put it: "We are not attracting people to us, asking them to join our group—to become proselytes. In passing on the message we are joining those who listen to the Gospel, in the expectation and the hope that there, once again, *people* will gather in the name of Jesus and that we shall be permitted to witness it."[20] Or, in the words of the great missionary, St. Paul, "We preach not ourselves, but Christ Jesus as Lord, with ourselves as your servants for Jesus' sake" (2 Cor 4:5).

The Witness of Baptism: Passage and Transformation

God's mission is to reconcile the world to himself. God has pursued this mission by calling and forming a people who shall be God's people. The means of calling, gathering, enlightening, and sanctifying God's people has been through the proclamation of the word and the celebration of the sacraments. This can be seen already in the history of Israel where Moses convenes the people to proclaim God's Torah and the people respond with the sacrifice that seals the covenantal relationship between Yahweh and Israel (Ex 24). This procedure was repeated in the reign of King Josiah, when the book of the Law was found and read to the king and the people, and the ritual response was the renewed Passover celebration (2 Kgs 22–23). In the book of Acts we also have a picture of a community of God's new people who "devoted themselves to the apostles' teaching and fellowship, to the breaking of bread and the prayers" (Acts 2:42).

The old Lutheran dogmatics distinguished between acts of worship which are *sacramental* (directed from God to the people) and *sacrificial* (directed from the people to God). The justification for these ritual acts of proclamation of the word in scripture, preaching, and sacramental sign-acts, is not only their usefulness for our personal spir-

61

itual formation but also the necessity for God's people to participate in God's mission. The proclamation of the word and the administration of the sacraments are the means by which God accomplishes his mission, because Christ is present in the word and sacraments and the Spirit works faith in those who hear and receive. Worship is not only what the people do; it is also what God does through the proclamation of the word and the administration of the sacraments.

Furthermore, the true worship of God is seen in the service of Christ to his heavenly Father. We who are called to be "in Christ" participate in his service and in his witness. Christ's service and witness is away from himself and to the Father; but it is on behalf of the world. That is exactly the model for the church's service and witness. We will see how this can be realized in terms of the witness of the worshiping community in its two most constitutive acts: baptism and the eucharist. We take up in this chapter the meaning of baptism in terms of witness.

Just as mission has a two-fold basis in Christology and pneumatology, so our understanding of baptism has to be worked out in relation both to Christ and to the Spirit.

In considering the christological aspects of baptism we may, for the sake of clarity, follow the order of Jesus' own ministry, noting the parallels between baptism and his birth, Jesus' baptism by John and ours, baptism and the death and resurrection of Jesus, and baptism and Jesus' high priestly office.

According to the author of the epistle to the Hebrews, "when Christ came into the world, he said . . . 'Lo, I have come to do thy will' " (Heb 10:5:9). The incarnation of the Son of God marks both his acceptance of his Father's will and the beginning of his mission. The rebirth of Christians in baptism is analogous to the birth of the Christ, in that their rebirth has to do with the acceptance of God's will and their participation in his mission. As the Son of God he is the one who has been sent; as the adopted sons and daughters of God Christians are also sent; their baptismal adoption refers to their participation in the mission of God. This comes into focus in the baptism of Jesus by John the Baptist.

The baptism of Christ was, to many of the church fathers, the foundation of Christian baptism. Particularly in the east, the feast of the Epiphany (which commemorated the baptism of Jesus) was the second great day in the church year for solemn public baptism—after Easter. As represented in the synoptic gospels, Christ's baptism was the occasion of his anointing with the Spirit, and so of his inauguration to and equiping for the office of messiah. His baptism thus marks an essential stage in his mission, and the temptations which follow indicate the development of his understanding of the nature of his task. This is brought out further by Luke when he records how Jesus went to his hometown synagogue at Nazareth and read from Isaiah, and then declared: "Today this scripture has been fulfilled in your hearing" (Lk 4:21). The passage in question begins, "The Spirit of the Lord is upon me, because he has anointed me to preach good news to the poor" (4:18). Christian baptism, through which we become partakers of the Spirit, is likewise an anointing with the Spirit to equip the Christian for mission; the individual is brought by the Spirit into the mission of God. So central a theme is this in the history and theology of baptism that an alternate name for the rite is "christening," which refers both to our identification with Christ in his mission and the act of anointing. The title "Christ" means "the anointed one."

The specific mission of the Christ points toward the cross; so then does his baptism. "I have a baptism to be baptized with; and how I am constrained until it is accomplished" (Lk 12:50). Paul connected Christian baptism very closely with the death of Jesus. "Do you not know that all of us who have been baptized into Christ Jesus

63

were baptized into his death?" (Rom 6:3) The candidate undergoes a co-death, a co-burial and a co-resurrection sacramentally with Christ. The church fathers pointed to the act of immersion in water as the ritual signification of this, and early Christian fonts were compared to tombs. Indeed, architectural evidence shows that baptismal pools were large enough for adults to descend into and to stand in while water was poured over the head. Pauline thought interpreted this ritual drowning as a death to sin and a rising to newness of life. But it would be a diminution of the apostle's thought to restrict this idea entirely to the concept of individual salvation. Rather, the individual was participating in the regeneration of the cosmos. "For the created universe waits with eager expectation for God's sons to be revealed" (Rom 8:19, *NEB*).

In commenting on the history of baptismal thought, in which the theological interest in baptism was "virtually disconnected from its cosmic significance" and reduced to liberation from original sin, Alexander Schmemann wrote:

> . . . both original sin and the liberation from it were given an extremely narrow and individual meaning. Baptism was understood as the means to assure the individual salvation of man's soul. No wonder that such an understanding of baptism led to a similar narrowing of the baptismal liturgy. From the act of the whole Church, involving the whole cosmos, it became a private ceremony, performed in a corner of the church by "private appointment," and in which the Church was reduced to the "minister of sacraments" and the cosmos to the three symbolic drops of water, considered as "necessary and sufficient" for the "validity" of the sacrament. *Validity* was the preoccupation—and not fullness, meaning, joy.[1]

It might be added that a major reason for the reduction of baptismal meaning and practice was the reduction of the size of the bath and the amount of water used. Another major reason for the reduction of baptismal meaning and practice was the separation of baptism from its paschal setting in the Easter Vigil. As Aidan Kavanagh has written,

> When the Easter Vigil "speaks" about initiation, it does so in terms of a veritable evangelization of the cosmos. Fire, wind, wax, bees, light and darkness, water, oil, nakedness, bread, wine, aromas, tough and graceful words and gestures: all these stand as a context without which what happens to one entering corporate faith in Jesus Christ dead and rising is only partially perceptible. The being and acts of Christ himself can even become constricted without regular paschal access to the full sweep of God's purpose that was being revealed long before the incarnation occurred. Because the discipline of Christian initiation is impoverished without regular access to the full paschal sweep of God's intents and accomplishments in Jesus Christ, the church becomes less than it is and may be, and so does the world.[2]

The emphasis in the idea of baptismal identification with Christ in his death and resurrection should be that through baptism the individual participates in Christ's death for the world, and the newness of life that is envisioned is one lived for others. As Paul wrote in 2 Corinthians 5:15, "he died for all, that those who live might live no longer for themselves but for him who for their sake died and was raised." Consequently, when we undergo baptismal death, we too die for all in union with Christ, and not just for ourselves. We may endorse the view of Rudolf Schnackenburg that "in Romans 6 Paul does not consider baptism as an external condition for entering into the fellowship of Christ, but he views it inwardly as an inclusion in that which happened to Christ himself."[3]

Since mission involves the reproduction of the pattern

65

of the incarnation, it is inseparable from suffering. The missionary life is the "dying life" poured out on behalf of others. This pattern is seen in Jesus, in his service and witness, *latreia* and *martyria*, and it is to be reproduced in those who follow him. As the author of 1 Peter writes, "For to this you have been called, because Christ also suffered for you, leaving you an example, that you should follow in his steps" (1 Pet 2:21). Baptism is a sacrament of identification with Christ—participation in his passion as he poured out his life for others. That which is sacramentally present in the cultic act is to be the pattern of the whole of life. So baptism, while unrepeatable, is never over and done with as far as the Christian is concerned. It is a beginning that has to be worked out throughout the whole of Christian life, so that we may steadily come to know Christ "and the power of his resurrection, and may share in his sufferings, becoming like him in his death" (Phil 3:10).

The historian of religions, Mircea Eliade, has shown that this pattern of death and resurrection is common to many initiation rites in human societies. It corresponds to the ordeals and crises which every person must undergo if one is to attain a responsible, genuine and creative life. "Man becomes *himself*," writes Eliade, "only after having solved a series of desperately difficult and even dangerous situations; that is, after having undergone 'tortures' and 'death,' followed by an awakening to another life, qualitatively different because regenerated."[4] We can see this pattern not only in rites of initiation into adulthood in primitive tribes and societies, but also in such modern rites of passage as education, vocational apprenticeship, military boot camp, etc. Eliade asserts that "initiation lies at the core of any genuine human life."[5] We should not be surprised, therefore, that Christian baptism has the character of a rite of initiation. In the ancient church this included the "ordeals" of the catechumenate in which candidates for baptism were formed in the life-style which the Christian community was called to exemplify. Even in situations where infant baptism is the prevalent practice, these "ordeals" are made up for in post-baptismal catechetical processes which may lead to confirmation as a solemn public affirmation of baptism. While we would not require confirmation as a necessary requirement for inclusion in the life of the church, we regard it as necessary for participation in the mission of the church. Lutheran congregational constitutions specify that only confirmed members may vote at congregational meetings or serve as members of church councils or on the committees of the congregation. We assume that adult candidates for baptism will receive the necessary instruction and spiritual formation to enable and equip them to participate fully in the life and mission of the church as a consequence of their baptism, without any subsequent catechesis and confirmation.

The consideration of baptism as a rite of initiation leads us to consider what one is initiated into. What one is initiated into is the community of faith in Jesus Christ dead and risen again, which has such an intimate relationship with him that it is called his "body." The issue I want to raise here is the character of this community whose members have sacramentally experienced death and resurrection with Christ. It surely cannot be a community that is concerned to create in the midst of life human enclaves which are havens from conflict and tension. Rather, it is to be numbered with those who are sent to be a suffering body in the world, showing forth the Lord's death until he comes. As Gibson Winter has written,

This community in Christ is not called to sacrifice its ministry of reconciliation in order to preserve its inner tranquility. This body is called to bear within itself the sufferings imposed upon it by a ministry of reconciliation within the broken communication of the world.[6]

This means that the most important thing that a witnessing church needs to learn is how to die, how to expend itself for others. A church which wants to hold fast to its own life, and will not let die all that does not serve its participation in the mission of God, is a church which has been unfaithful to its baptismal foundation.

A church which is faithful to its baptismal calling will cultivate its priestly service and witness to God. In Hebrews, Christ is named "Apostle and High Priest of our confession" (3:1), and the conjunction of these two titles brings together the ideas of mission and priesthood. Insofar as Christians are members of Christ, they share in a royal priesthood (1 Peter 2:9). This text in 1 Peter has long been interpreted in the sense that each person is his or her own priest and does not need any other mediator between himself or herself and God. In a significant dissertation, John H. Elliott has demonstrated that the "royal priesthood" metaphor in 1 Peter is an extension of the "kingdom of priests" metaphor in Exodus 19, as it was applied to Israel.[7] The fact that Israel was called a "kingdom of priests" did not negate the presence of a special priestly ministry in Israel; nor does the fact that the church is called a "royal priesthood" negate the role of the office of presbyter in the church. In fact, 1 Peter was written by one who exhorted "the elders among you, as a fellow elder and a witness of the sufferings of Christ as well as a partaker in the glory that is to be revealed: Tend the flock of God that is in your charge . . ." (1 Pet 5:1–2). So how are we to understand the priestly vocation of baptized Christians?

First, the priesthood belongs to the Christian community as a whole and is to be exercised by the community, not for itself but on behalf of all humankind. Secondly, this priesthood derives from the new covenant which has been inaugurated by the sacrifice of Christ. The community of Jesus the messiah has been established in the last days that God may be revealed through it to the whole world. The royal priesthood fulfills the purpose of its consecration by bringing God to the world and the world to God. It does this liturgically by offering the world itself to God in a sacrifice of prayer, praise, and thanksgiving—the world as represented by the bread and wine, our money, food and clothing for the needy, etc.; and by interceding on behalf of the world. But it will know for whom and what to pray only when it is involved in the affairs of the world and in the needs of its members. The true priesthood of the faithful is exercised, not when lay persons take upon themselves the pastor's responsibility to publicly preach the gospel and administer the sacraments, but when they diligently and robustly participate in the prayers of the faithful and the offering of gifts.

Baptism is consecration or ordination to this priestly ministry. Thus, Tertullian could compare the baptismal anointing to the anointing of priests in the old covenant. Jerome spoke of baptism as the "lay priesthood." Augustine asserted the priestly character of the faithful, and associated it with the high priestly ministry of Christ. The priestly function of Christians, conferred by their baptismal ordination, is not only to be associated with the high priesthood of Christ, but also with that priesthood which is natural to all humankind. As Schmemann wrote, "Man was created priest of the world, the one who offers the world to God in a sacrifice of love and praise and who, through this eternal eucharist, bestows the divine love upon the world."[8] But man has lost his true priesthood because he sees the world as an end in itself; he no longer beholds it as transparent to God. So his communion with God does not embrace the whole world, but is narrowed down to the "religious" sphere, since the world is no longer the sacrament of God's presence. The death of Christ was the end of priestly *religion* and the beginning of priestly *life*, because he was killed by the priests and raised from the dead by the God who vindicated his true priestly service and witness. Those who are baptized into Christ share in this priestly ministry. "If there are priests in the Church," wrote Schmemann, "if there is the priestly vocation in it, it is precisely in order to reveal to each vocation its priestly essence, to make the whole life of all men the liturgy of the Kingdom, to reveal the Church as the royal priesthood of the redeemed world."[9]

At this point we turn from the christological basis of mission to the pneumatological, for it is the Spirit who empowers and equips the church for mission by bestowing on its members those gifts which are needed for its tasks. It is from this perspective that we should try to understand the *charismata* or grace-gifts of which Paul speaks in 1 Corinthians 12–14.

These gifts stem from the saving work of Christ in whom the grace (*charis*) of God was revealed and actualized. They are mediated to the faithful through his indwelling Spirit: "All these are inspired by one and the same Spirit, who apportions to each one individually as he wills" (1 Cor 12:11). They are, in fact, outward signs of the Spirit's inward activity. These "manifestations" of the Spirit are not given to the individual to glorify himself; they are not endowments for individual self-expression nor are they primarily concerned with fostering the individual's relation with God, but with building up the church. That's why Paul considers prophesying or proclaiming a higher gift than speaking in tongues. "He who speaks in tongues edifies himself, but he who prophesies edifies the church" (14:4).

But to what end is the church built up? That it may be a fitting instrument to be used by God in the prosecution of his mission to reconcile humanity to himself. The *charismata* are elements in the mission of God since God's gifts are always at the same time tasks laid upon us. Because the church is involved in God's mission it is incumbent upon the church to recognize true spiritual gifts among its members and to provide means whereby those gifts may be employed in nurturing the members of the body and reaching out to those who are not a part of the body.

If one were to select a single, comprehensive term to describe the Spirit's activity, the term that suggests itself is "sanctification." Sanctification is to be associated with the concept of holiness, which means that which belongs to God. Since God claims as his own those who are baptized, the baptized are holy people and are expected to live as though they do belong to God. As St. Paul puts it, "you were washed, you were sanctified, you were justified in the name of the Lord Jesus Christ and in the Spirit of our God" (1 Cor 6:11). Sanctification is as much a gift of God as justification, and both are signified by baptism. Gustav Wingren suggests how sanctification can be expressed.

> The fellowship of the Church flourishes in its purest form when it suffers and yet does not pay heed to its own distress but to the needs of the world around. . . . When its members make holiness a thing to be grasped in the sacraments with others who have similarly sought it, they are again "in Adam." Holiness is then conceived to be a quality which gains in purity in proportion as the Church shuts itself off from ordinary human relationships. Humanity then disappears from the Church.[10]

In other words, holiness is not something the church has to seek by cultivating a religious life apart from secular involvements. Quite the contrary: Christians are already holy by virtue of the fact that God adopts them as his own holy baptism. And since baptism is incorporation into a community which is called to participate in the mission of God for the sake of the world, Christians are to be found in the midst of worldly activities, exercising a transforming influence on the persons, institutions, and tasks with whom and in which they are involved.

71

I would hesitate to call this "secularization," as the theologians of secularism did a couple of decades ago. I appreciate their concern that the cross of Christ ended any dichotomy between the sacred and the profane, and that the church has betrayed the mission of God whenever it has fostered some kind of divorce between the religious and the secular. The *saeculum*—the world—is precisely the object of God's mission. But as the cross of Christ is an indictment against religion, it is also an indictment against the secular. It was "this world" which crucified Christ, both in its religious and in its secular manifestations. God's resurrection of the crucified messiah was to proclaim something which transcends both the sacred and the profane—the eschatological or the end-time reality. As the death and resurrection of Christ inaugurated the end-time, so the Spirit of Christ is the down payment on the new age (2 Cor 1:22). For Luke the Spirit's descent is a fulfillment of Joel's prophecy that "in the last days" God would pour out his Spirit on all flesh (Acts 2:17). To be led by that Spirit to baptismal rebirth and to receive the gifts of that Spirit in the baptismal anointing and laying on of hands is to be thrust into the eschatological crisis which is a consequence of God's decision to act now in the mission of his Son. Those who are baptized into Christ's death and resurrection and receive the down payment on the future kingdom of God by the pouring out of the gift of the Holy Spirit constitute together the eschatological community whose vocation is to model the new creation in the midst of the old one.

I ought to stop here, because any attempt to spin out the consequences of the eschatological interpretation of baptism is bound to put me on dangerous ground. But the question begs to be asked: *should everyone be baptized?* We have assumed for a long time in church history that every person ought to be baptized. In the culture and society known as Christendom it was inconceivable that anyone would not be baptized (except a stiff-necked Jew or a heathen Turk, as they said). Baptism was tantamount to full citizenship in many of the so-called "Christian nations" of Europe from roughly the end of the ancient period in western history until well into the modern era. That legacy lives on in the many children who are presented for baptism by parents who do not participate in the life of the church as it pursues the mission of God. What to do about this is probably the most vexing problem pastors face. But just for that reason we must constantly wrestle with it. Let me raise it again by relating this datum.

R. E. O. White has questioned whether even the great commission in Matthew's gospel should be interpreted as meaning that every person is summoned to baptism. "A change of gender in the objects of the verbs [make disciples . . . baptize . . . teach] suggests that while the discipling is applied to 'all nations,' the baptizing and teaching is for those [disciples] who accept the discipling: the gospel is for all, baptism for disciples."[11] In other words, all are called to discipleship, but only those who heed the call are baptized.

No matter what one thinks of this interpretation, it is the case that the church has been more or less discriminate in its baptismal policy. It has never turned the hoses on whole communities for a mass baptism (although the baptism of the Saxon tribes in the Rhine at sword point under orders from Charlemagne came close). Nevertheless, Tertullian, who was a witness to the practice of infant baptism at the beginning of the third century, was opposed to it. "Let them be made Christians when they have become competent to know Christ. Why should innocent infancy come with haste to the remission of sins? Shall we take less cautious action in this than we take in worldly matters? Shall one who is not trusted with earthly property be entrusted with heavenly?"[12] It is from Tertullian that we have the slogan, "Christians are made, not born." His contemporary, Hippolytus of Rome, was a witness to the arduous process of making Christians. While he was also a witness to the practice of infant baptism, and did not seem bothered by it, he imposed a three-year waiting policy on adults (although, he added, "it is not the time that is judged, but the conduct").[13] Many Christians in the fourth and fifth centuries were enrolled as catechumens in childhood, but were not baptized until they reached adulthood. Augustine was baptized at the age of 33. Ambrose, the great bishop of Milan whose preaching had been influential on Augustine, was baptized and ordained a bishop on the same day. He had delayed baptism because he had been a magistrate before his sudden election as bishop. Some political leaders, such as the Emperor Constantine, delayed baptism until they were near death, even though they were Christian catechumens. Their concern was not to compromise the eschatological witness of the church by their involvement in the daily affairs of this world. It was a recognition that baptism entailed participation in the mission of God.

Perhaps this is a scrupulosity we would not want and could not observe in the church today. But whatever pastoral decisions we make in our contemporary baptismal policy, we must clearly understand that baptism is initiation into a community which is called to participate in the mission of God. Those who are not interested in participating in this mission, or who do not envision their children doing so, and who are unwilling to see that their children are equipped by the catechetical program of the church to participate in this mission, should not be encouraged to bring themselves or their children to the font. Baptism is the public work of the whole church; it is not primarily a family-cultural rite. One way to move away from the family-cultural captivity of the sacrament, which is a legacy of Christendom, is for parishes to institute the ancient practice of baptizing at specified times of the church year. All baptisms would be celebrated at these baptismal festivals.[14] Connecting baptism with the church-year calendar would reinforce its missional dimensions. Baptism at Epiphany (or the Sunday after the Epiphany, the Baptism of our Lord) would proclaim God's adoption of new sons and daughters who will be identified with the mission of his only-begotten Son. Baptism at the Easter Vigil would proclaim our participation in Christ's passover from death to life. Baptism at Pentecost would proclaim our reception of the gifts of the Holy Spirit to empower us for ministry —our ordination to the vocation and mission of priesthood. Baptism on or about Holy Cross Day on September 14 would proclaim our call to a life of suffering service for the sake of the kingdom of God—our vocation to martyrdom. There is more to be gained than lost by instituting this practice, if we think of the church in terms of its missionary responsibilities rather than its institutional necessities.

The Witness of the Eucharist: The World as Sacrament

Although I am treating the eucharist in a chapter separated from the one devoted to baptism, I would not want this division to obscure their essential interrelatedness. The two sacraments can be understood fully only in terms of their interdependence. This can be underscored if we recall that baptism is the church's rite of initiation, and ask: into what is one initiated? The answer is: into the eucharistic fellowship. This relationship between baptism as initiation and the eucharist as incorporation is illustrated by the names of the two chief parts of the liturgy: the liturgy of the catechumens (the service of readings and instruction) and the liturgy of the faithful (the service of holy communion, from the offertory on). The baptismal liturgies of the ancient church all culminated in the first reception of holy communion. Never in the history of the church have the unbaptized been admitted to the fellowship of the altar. In fact, in the ancient church the catechumens were dismissed before the liturgy of the faithful began. There is a remnant of this in the Eastern Orthodox liturgy in which the deacon shouts, "The doors, The doors," before the offertory begins. It simply never would have occurred to the ancient church to broadcast or televise the service of holy communion, had such media been available.

From the vantage point of eucharistic fellowship, it needs to be asked whether baptism really is the rite of initiation if something else in addition to baptism is required for participation in the Lord's supper. Whatever that something else might be—e.g., a catechetical program leading to confirmation, repentant self-examination, first confession, or all three—it will stand in competition with baptism and undermine the doctrine of justification by grace alone through faith. And as long as baptism alone is regarded as the missionary sacrament, the eucharist will be regarded only as an optional extra for the especially devout.

However, there is a sense in which the missionary mandate to go to the nations, teaching the observance of Christ's *torah*, making disciples, and baptizing them in the name of the Father and of the Son and of the Holy Spirit, is dependent on the eucharistic presence of Christ. Carrying out the great commission is possible only in the context of the promise, "I am with you always. . . ." If this word of promise is not somehow embodied, then it is false and Christ's presence is an illusion. If Christ's presence is not real, then it is unreal. If Christ is not really present, then he is really absent. But in fact the faith of the church has perceived Christ's real presence embodied in the eucharistic bread and cup. In the history of Christian mission it has not just been the case that converts are brought, by baptism, into the eucharistic assembly. It has also been the case that whole eucharistic assemblies were planted in a missionary territory and served as centers of missionary activity. The entire thousand-year evangelization of Europe proceeded on this basis.

Thus, in the sacramental economy it is imperative to see the relationship between baptism and the eucharist also for the Christian mission. J. G. Davies has proposed four areas of interdependence between baptism and the eucharist.

I.   Baptism is ordination to the royal priesthood and acceptance into the covenant, both priesthood and covenant being understood in terms of mission. The eucharist renews both the ordination and the covenant.

II.   Baptism, with its pattern of life and death, initiates us into mission. The eucharist reestablishes us in this pattern.

III.   Baptism includes us in the obedience of Christ and so in his mission. The eucharist renews our commitment to God and so to mission.

IV.   Baptism is an eschatological sacrament and so is the eucharist; both are intimately related in this sense to mission.[1]

In the previous chapter we highlighted baptism as ordination to the royal priesthood of the redeemed. This baptismal ordination is reaffirmed and, in fact, is exercized, in the eucharistic liturgy, above all in the offertory. What does a priest do? A priest offers gifts and intercedes on behalf of others. In the eucharistic liturgy the faithful offer the world to God in a sacrifice of love and praise. They offer their petitions on behalf of the whole church and all people according to their needs. They offer their tangible gifts, as expressing their self-offering, by appeal to the unique sacrifice of Christ as the only basis on which they dare to stand before God and offer anything to him. I want to focus here on the prayers and on the offering of gifts.

The prayers of the faithful, included both in the general intercessions and sometimes in the intercessions of the great thanksgiving, are a participation in Christ's priesthood. Christ's high priestly office is one of intercession (Rom 8:34; Heb 7:25). In the Old Testament the high priest was the people's representative. Christ is our representative before the Father in heaven. But because we have "put on Christ" in holy baptism, we also participate in his priestly ministry and stand before God the Father as the world's representatives, exercising the royal and priestly ministry given to Adam and Eve in the beginning. We bring the concerns of the world to God in prayer because the world cannot pray for itself, and we do this in the faith that we mean to exert some influence on God on behalf of those for whom we pray. In reformed Roman Catholic, Episcopal, Lutheran, United Methodist and Presbyterian liturgies the space for intercession is left open so that it may be filled as is deemed appropriate and sometimes the faithful are encouraged to add their own petitions and thanksgivings spontaneously. We note that the intercessions are often led by an assisting minister or a deacon who represents the laity, or the priesthood of believers. In the ancient church deacons led the intercessions because they were involved in those areas of ministry on behalf of the church in which prayer was urgently needed.

In these reformed liturgies, the intercessions conclude the liturgy of the word. The greeting of peace follows in all but the Roman liturgy as the hinge into the liturgy of the eucharistic meal. This is the peace of reconciliation. If there is not real reconciliation of divided factions in the eucharistic fellowship, the church cannot function as a sign of the new creation of reconciled humanity.

After the greeting of peace, there is a collection of gifts, usually of money but sometimes also of food and clothing for the relief of the poor and needy. Paul twice referred to this collection as *koinonia*, "fellowship" (2 Cor 9:13; Rom 15:26). It is not a question of what money is but what it becomes in relation to its final reference, and that reference is building up the fellowship of the church. The funds collected extend the mission of the church both at home and abroad. They are also signs of the self-giving of the members of Christ, and thus a means of identity be-

79

tween Christ and his people. This is emphasized in 2 Corinthians 8:9, "You know the grace of our Lord Jesus Christ, that though he was rich, yet for your sakes he became poor, that you through his poverty might become rich." This is not just an illustration of the need for charity but the very foundation of the *koinonia* of giving. Our response in gratitude to Christ's self-impoverishment must be self-giving, for giving to others is giving to Christ who gave himself for us. Christians therefore give with liberality, i.e., without ulterior motive, without thought of gain (8:2), having first given themselves to God in complete surrender (8:5). This is the ministry (*diakonia*) required of followers of Christ (9:1), who "came not to be served, but to serve" (Mk 10:45).

Gifts of bread and wine are also offered to God. They are the essential matter of the eucharistic oblation, and more than anything else they represent the world itself. "The world," according to Schmemann, "was created as the 'matter,' the material of an all-embracing eucharist, and man was created as the priest of this cosmic sacrament."[2] The Christian eucharist declares the eucharistic nature of the whole creation. It witnesses to the world itself as a sacrament—the means of God's presence to and communion with his creatures.

The bread and wine are presented to be consecrated or sanctified. This is to enable humanity to understand that all matter can be the means of communion with God. Consecration is often misunderstood to consist of making sacred that which was profane. It has also been misunderstood to be a survival, within a religious enclave, of that which has been holy from the beginning. The more accurate view, as Louis Bouyer points out, is that consecration is "simple acceptance on the part of man of the divine having its own way, a 'liturgy,' that is, a 'service,' through which he hands himself over and submits himself to the

will on high."[3] The eucharistic consecration, far from expressing a separation from the world, the secular, indicates
the unity of worship and everyday life. Moreover, the
form of consecration is thanksgiving. By making eucharist
(i.e., giving thanks) the church acknowledges the true nature of the things humankind receives from God and declares them to be what God intended them to be from the
beginning: his gracious gifts to us and our means of communion with him. This is why the great thanksgiving or
eucharistic prayer is also the great act of proclamation in
the liturgy.

Consecration is not sacralization—a separation of
persons and things from the world in order to place them
in a religious compartment. It is not secularization either
—the flattening out of reality to a material dimension.
Consecration is an eschatological or teleological act—an
orientation of life and the world to its true purpose or end.
In the presentation of the bread and wine, all industry,
whether of farm or factory, is dedicated to God's use. We
do not present just grapes and grain, but wine and bread
which are a microcosm of our present industrial system.
The grain and grapes have been harvested in diverse parts
of the world with implements forged of metals mined in
different parts of the globe and powered by all sorts of
fuels. They have been transported by a vast system of ship-
ping, imported by means of an elaborate method of international exchange, processed by related trades, and finally
distributed by another network of transportation and re-
tailing. We have brought the world into the presence of
God, offered it to his use, and by this act proclaimed what
it shall be from God's end of things. Where contemporary
life splits into segments—production/consumption, fac-
tory/residential areas—the offertory reveals its basic unity in the purpose of God. In an increasingly depersona-
lized world, in which people are seen to exist for the

manipulation of things, the bread and wine are transformed into things which exist for the use of God in his service to humankind.

The offertory is thus a paradigm of mission because God's mission is reconciliation. The eucharist, celebrated in a condition of *shalom*, of peace and well-being, is a sign of reconciliation. The sacramental elements themselves are signs of reconciliation, since the flesh of Christ is given "for the life of the world" (Jn 6:51) and the blood of Christ is poured out "for many for the forgiveness of sins" (Mt 26:28). As the first-fruits of the kingdom of God, the church is to manifest the reality of reconciliation in its own life together. The eucharists that manifest instead class divisions or color barriers are not a part of the "ministry of reconciliation" (2 Cor 5:18). The eucharist is often celebrated, of course, as though it had to do only with the reconciliation of Christians (and there's no doubt that we need it!). But relating the eucharist to baptism reminds us that it has to do with the reconciliation of God and the world. We give thanks because Christ has given himself for the life of the world—of that we are witnesses. Christ himself is the one who "before Pontius Pilate witnessed the good confession" (1 Tim 6:13). This is the earthly counterpart of his confession of humankind before the Father: "every one therefore who shall confess me before men, him will I also confess before my Father who is in heaven" (Mt 10:32). So Christians confess him and witness to him in cultic acts and in their everyday lives so that Christ may confess both them and the world before the Father. Every eucharistic gathering is therefore an act of witness. But it is a witness that must also be expressed in a life-style, and this brings us to the second of Davies' theses on the relationship between baptism and the eucharist in terms of mission.

We have said that baptism draws us into the pattern of the incarnation, specifically the death and resurrection of

Christ. The word to be stressed here is *pattern*. As we have learned from Luther's *Small Catechism*, baptism signifies a *daily* drowning of the old self so that *daily* the new self may arise who will live before God forever. The early Christian writings on martyrdom stressed that by means of the eucharist Christians are identified with Christ in his death and resurrection because it is a partaking, a sharing, a *koinonia*, a *communio* in his passion. The body and blood symbolize the dedicated victim and the surrendered life. Baptism initiates us into the sacrificial life of Christ; the eucharist renews us in this life. The cross is central to the eucharist. In the eucharistic memorial we remember that he "made there (by his one oblation of himself once offered) a full, perfect, and sufficient sacrifice, oblation, and satisfaction, for the sins of the whole world" (in the incomparable language of *The Book of Common Prayer*). The act of sacramental eating and drinking thus becomes a proclamation of the Lord's death until he comes (1 Cor 11:26). This is the same as the priestly community declaring the wonderful deeds of God (1 Pet 2:9). The act of proclamation of the cross is at the heart of both worship and witness, and it is a proclamation made by laying one's life on the line as well as by making speeches.

If we accept the necessity of a eucharistic pattern in mission, this will have profound consequences for understanding the church. Gibson Winter has suggested that in the past there have been two main ideas about the church —the church as cultic community and the church as a confessing fellowship. He argues that these must be supplemented with a third concept of the church: the church as servant.[4] This leads to a third consideration: that baptism and the eucharist include us in the obedience of Christian mission. The stance of the servant is to obey orders. Jesus constantly sought to do his Father's will in pursuing the mission given to him. This obedience led him even to death on a cross (Phil 2:8). Obedience in the context of the

83

eucharist is to "do" what is comprehended in the domini-
cal command, "Do this for my remembrance" (1 Cor
11:25, 26).

What is comprehended in the mandate to "do this" is:
taking bread and a cup of wine, giving thanks over them,
and eating the bread and drinking from the cup.[5] In other
words, the faithful are to observe the eucharistic rite; and
intrinsic ingredients of this rite include bread to be
broken, a cup of wine to be shared, and a prayer of thanksgiving which articulates the saving acts of God in Christ so
as to present these to the Father with an appeal for their
benefits to us. The eucharistic tradition has used the tech-
nical terms *anamnesis* and *epiclesis* to designate these
aspects of eucharistic praying.[6] The mandate to "do this"
is not burdensome, and therefore it is scandalous that
Christian communities have failed variously to use bread
and/or a cup of wine, to pray a thanksgiving, or to eat
and/or drink.

The mandate specifies that the eucharistic rite be observed "often" (1 Cor 11:26), but does not say how frequently. The evidence of Christian antiquity shows that a
pattern of Sunday celebration was established early and
universally.[7] By the fifth century, however, the emphasis
on the holiness of the consecrated elements combined
with requirements of abstinence discouraged frequent reception.[8] By the end of the Middle Ages in the west Christians had to be required to receive once a year at Easter.
The Protestant reformers Martin Luther, Philip Me-
lanchthon, Martin Bucer, and John Calvin wanted Christians to receive communion more frequently than the
obligatory once a year or even four times a year. In the
Reformed churches insistence that the whole congregation
participate impeded the practice of celebrating the Lord's
supper more than four times a year or once a month. In the
Lutheran churches the people were exhorted to commune
as often as possible, after careful preparation, and the

Lord's supper was celebrated whenever there were communicants. Progress was being made until the eighteenth century when the Pietist emphasis on repentant self-examination engendered scruples against unworthy reception and the rationalist depreciation of the supernatural fostered a low regard for the sacraments. John Wesley favored weekly celebrations of the Lord's supper but conditions, especially on the American frontier, with scattered settlements and the absence of ordained ministers, militated against this practice. The Disciples of Christ were able to institute weekly celebrations of the Lord's supper by dispensing with the need for ordained ministers to preside. The time has now come to restore this ancient practice, not just because of our deep human need for the grace of the sacrament, but also in the interests of the life and mission of the church. The ecclesial body of Christ is built up by participation (*koinonia*) in the sacramental body of Christ (1 Cor 10:16).

This brings us to Davies' fourth point: both baptism and the eucharist are eschatological sacraments. Baptism initiates us into the life and mission of the eschatological community. Every eucharist marks the appearance or *parousia* of the risen and ascended One who comes again to judge the living and the dead. Participation in holy communion is not participation in a mythical event which enables religious devotees to escape from the threats of historical existence by transcending time and place.[9] Rather, holy communion locates us in the history of God's dealing with his people and their destiny in his kingdom. This is why the eucharistic celebration is *prolepsis* as well as *anamnesis*—a "foretaste of the feast to come." But how do we understand our present situation over against that future of God?

There have been two untenable eschatological strategies. In the case of a realized eschatology the kingdom of God is manifested within the elect community, and this can easily result in triumphalism and self-righteousness on a communal level. In the case of apocalypticism, the kingdom of God is coming in the future and the elect have to huddle together to keep themselves pure and undefiled while they await its unexpected arrival and the world pursues its headlong course to perdition. Both eschatological perspectives are present in the Bible and have been manifested in Christian history. But each is inadequate because it represents only one side of the now/not yet paradox of Christian life. An inaugurated eschatology preserves the paradox. It believes that the last times have begun in the death and resurrection of Jesus Christ; the kingdom of God has been inaugurated, but it has not yet come in its fullness or triumph. Nevertheless, it is operative in the world and one may point to signs of the kingdom in the world as well as in the church. The eucharist is celebrated as the anticipation of the messianic feast of the kingdom when "many will come from east and west, and from north and south, and sit at table in the kingdom of God" (Lk 13:29). The keynote of the eucharistic celebration is gladness (Acts 2:46f.), since it not only looks back to the cross but forward to the joy and peace of the kingdom. To participate in the eucharist is to live out the future in the present on the basis of the past accomplishments of Christ.

The presence of the crucified and risen One in the eucharist is his declaration that the future belongs to his brothers and sisters. Who are these? Not just the sheep in this sheepfold. ". . . I have other sheep, that are not of this fold; I must bring them also, and they will heed my voice. So there shall be one flock, one shepherd" (Jn 10:16). Christ's presence is bound up with mission, which is itself an eschatological process giving meaning to the present by opening up the future on the basis of Christ's work. "Mission," says R. K. Orchard, "is participation in the Event which stands on the boundary line between the life of this age and the life of the age to come."[10] It is the same with the eucharist. According to Louis Bouyer, "The world of the sacraments, the world into which the liturgy introduces us, is not a world in its own right, standing aloof from the world of ordinary living. It is rather the meeting point of the world of the resurrection with this very world of ours in which we must live, suffer, and die."[11] The eucharist is therefore a summons to full historical existence by participating in the eschatological mission of God.

This is perhaps best expressed by the image of the church receiving the body of Christ to become his body in the world. "Because there is one loaf, we who are many are one body, for we all partake of the same loaf" (1 Cor 10:17). These words refer to the union between the members of the body and each other with their head. In patristic thought this was elaborated to the effect that it is by feeding on the sacramental body of Christ that the church becomes the body of Christ in the world. This is particularly emphasized by St. Augustine, who said that "the spiritual benefit which is here understood is unity, that being joined to his body and made his members we may be what we receive" (*Sermo* 57:7). Alexander Schmemann put it this way: "The eucharist, transforming the church into what it is, transforms it into mission."[12] It simply *is* our mission to be the body of Christ in the world —to be an example of the new creation inaugurated in his death and resurrection.

To envision the relationship between eucharist and mission correctly, we must now repeat an emphasis that has been made in several of these chapters: the necessity as opposed to the usefulness of worship. If we think in terms of usefulness, then worship is simply a good preparation for being sent out to do mission. Worship is seen as providing a source of power to enable Christians to witness to Christ in their daily lives. How often has it been said that the word and the sacraments strengthen us for mission, in terms of cause and effect. Against this it has to be affirmed that worship is not a means to mission, it is an aspect of mission—God's mission. We do not prepare for mission by worshiping, and we do not turn worship into an evangelistic tool. Rather, worship is the occasion for God and his people to encounter one another, by means of God's sacramental gifts and his people's sacrificial response. We should not ask how is *our* worship to be related to *our* mission, but how is the worship in which *God* participates related to *his* mission? If worship is, in fact, a part of God's mission, then there is no separation of worship and mission from God's side. Then from our side our worship is a way of participating in the mission of God, just as our witness is.

This conclusion has certain consequences for the life of the church today. We have heard much in recent years about the need to renew the church for mission or of the possibility of liturgical renewal resulting in a reformation of the church. But these notions are open to the same objection: they stem from the utilitarian approach and tend to perpetuate a dichotomy between worship and mission. They are cause-and-effect arguments. Renew the church —and then we can proceed to mission. Reform the liturgy —and then a renewed church can begin its task. We hear the same argument for church unity. Let us be one—then we can engage in effective mission. But if the church only exists in mission, then it is only in mission that it can be renewed. The church is engaging in mission when it worships. As its worship is renovated, its mission will be renovated. The church is engaged in mission when it addresses the gospel to those in need, and provides necessary services to the poor and destitute. As it recommits itself to these acts of witness and service, it will be recommitted to mission. Any renewal of any missionary activity will contribute to the renewal of the church.

This has an important bearing on liturgical reform. The point of reform is not to restyle our worship to make it a better evangelism tool by making it more of a mirror of our cultural fads and fancies. The point of liturgical reform is to make our worship more reflective of what the church is called to be as the people of God, the body of Christ, the herald of the kingdom, the sacrament of Christ's presence in the world, the servant of God.[13] There is an essential connection between liturgy and ecclesiology. The liturgy should be styled so that it is done by the whole church—clergy and people, young and old, rich and poor, black and white, men and women, learned and unlearned, each contributing the gift he or she has to the building up of the whole body. This does not mean that the laity should usurp the pastor's role as preacher and presider. Nor should the pastor usurp the people's liturgical roles. Nor should there be quota systems that smack of law enforcement, but rather a spiritual freedom for each to contribute what he or she is able and to be encouraged to do so by the other members of the body. We need a variety of gifts: the gifts of hospitality, of singing, of reading in public, of praying, of offering, of making banners, of baking bread, of arranging space—whatever the gift may be, there is a place for it in the liturgy. A liturgy in which all this is happening is a paradigm of the new, reconciled humanity.

There should be no lack of confidence that God's mission of reconciliation is being accomplished in the liturgy of word and sacrament. The preaching of the word of God and the administration of the sacraments of Christ are means of grace, ways in which God accomplishes his mission, and therefore an essential part of the church's mission. It has been an essential missionary strategy to invite people into the assembly for word and sacrament where they may hear and experience the proclamation and celebration of the gospel. One tactic that has sometimes been used in the church's missionary enterprise is to establish communities of word and sacrament in territories to be evangelized, so that this ministry and assembly would be intact when people are invited into it.

But the historic liturgy has also concluded by launching the church into mission. In fact, the name "mass" comes from the old words of dismissal at the end of the Roman liturgy—*Ite missa est* (a phrase which is virtually untranslatable).[14] Reformed eucharistic liturgies have included an act of dismissal such as: Assistant—"Go in peace. Serve the Lord." Congregation—"Thanks be to God." The words of the Song of Simeon, the *Nunc dimittis*, sung after the reception of communion in some classical Lutheran liturgies point to the reality of what has been experienced in word and sacrament.

> My own eyes have seen the salvation
>> which you have prepared in the sight of every people:
> A light to reveal you to the nations
>> and the glory of your people Israel.

Or, in the words of the Byzantine liturgy: "We have seen the true light, we have partaken of the Holy Spirit." It is as witnesses of this light—the presence of Christ—that the faithful are dismissed and return to the never-ending mission of the church in the world. Because we know what we have experienced, the goodness of the Lord which has been tasted and seen (Ps 34:8), we are now *competent* to be witnesses of the grace of God.

Invitational Evangelism: Hospitality and Inculturation

Because the proclamation of the word and the administration of the sacraments are a part of God's mission of reconciling the world to himself, it is right and proper to invite others, without the arrogance of proselytism, to come to church. For "church" is nothing other than the assembly called out of the world to be constituted as God's people by God's word and the sacraments of Christ. A paradigm for invitational evangelism is seen in John 1:35ff. John the Baptist points his disciples away from himself and toward "the Lamb of God." When those disciples express an interest in where Jesus is staying (*menein* can mean "to lodge," but it can also mean "to abide" or "to dwell together with"), Jesus says "come and see." Andrew first gets his brother Simon, whom Jesus renames Cephas. Then Jesus found Philip, and Philip invited Nathanael—also with the words "come and see." Those looking for the promised One are invited to explore the possibilities offered by Jesus. As they make their home with him they arrive at life-changing and redemptive insights.

When we invite people to make their home with Jesus in the community of his people, we must be prepared to receive such guests with appropriate hospitality. Congregations have not always heeded the biblical mandate to show hospitality to strangers. Out of its Semitic heritage, Israel was to remember the rules of hospitality. "When a stranger sojourns with you in your land, you shall not do him wrong, and you shall love him as yourself;"—and then the reason for Israel's hospitality is added—"for you were strangers in the land of Eygpt" (Lev 19:33–34). When a temple was finally built for Yahweh in Jerusalem, it was "the Lord's house" and the Lord was clearly the host of the place. Therefore even foreigners were to be accorded a place in the temple precincts (I Kgs 8:41–43). The same concern for hospitality to strangers passed into the Christian community: "Contribute to the needs of the saints, practice hospitality. . . ." (Rom 12:13). The practice of hospitality has been demonstrated in the history of Christianity, from the three days of free room and board provided to the traveling prophets in the late first-century church manual known as *The Didache* to the overnight accommodations provided by the medieval monasteries. So indelibly ingrained was the practice of hospitality in the consciousness of Christians, that even hermits in the desert set aside their solitude to provide for visitors. And if the press of visitors became too great, rather than turn them away and thereby refuse hospitality the hermits simply went farther into the desert.

The survival, let alone the growth, of our congregations depends on attracting visitors. But this does not mean that practices of hospitality are intact. Ben Johnson correctly alerts us to the fact that not all congregations want to grow. He writes: "Nearly all churches state verbally their desire to grow. Often, however, their profession means 'we want to grow if persons will conform to the traditions and values of the church, but we do not want to grow if it requires change.' "[1] Growth without change is impossible. People instinctively realize this and therefore there can be a natural resistance to showing hospitality to strangers. It is caused by the realization that newcomers represent a potential threat to their way of life. In our neighborhoods, particularly in places where a way of life is being assiduously clung to, newcomers are "scoped out" to see if they will "fit in." The same defensiveness characterizes churches, and has been the case from the very beginning in spite of the fact that Christianity was a missionary cult. The influx of Gentile converts represented a theological as well as a sociological threat to the original core of Jewish Christianity, and much of the New Testament is devoted to dealing with the integration of Jews and Greeks. The same dynamics go into play when Afro-American, Hispanic, or Oriental people come into all-white, Euro-American congregations; or when Yuppies invade an older ethnic congregation.

I have become skeptical of the notion that many of our congregations are ready and willing to invite people to church or to put out the welcome mat. Patrick Keifert has put his finger on the reason for this: our model of the church in recent years has become that of the "family of God" and we have lost a sense of the church as a public place and worship as a public event.[2]

Most of us are wary of strangers, particularly if the strangers are not like ourselves. Put a shabbily-dressed black man on a quiet residential street in a mostly white suburb, and some housewife is going to call the police. This is just the way we are. And it seems to me that we are less and less willing to deal with strangers. This has affected public life. We don't like to go to public places unless we feel comfortable in them, and the level of comfort is probably determined by the experience of the number of other people at the event who will be like ourselves. We don't like strangers, and we don't like being strangers.

And we transfer this to our church life. Oh, to be sure, we like to maintain a warm and open atmosphere in church, in which we clearly intend to welcome the stranger—if he or she is someone like ourselves. But the fact is that we are not hospitable to strangers because we think of the church as the "family of God," and, believe it or not, families are not easy to break into. We who are a part of the "family" know what we're doing here, but the outsider doesn't know—and most congregations don't provide a lot of help. Until congregations understand their buildings to be public places, and their worship services to be public events, we will continue to exclude "outsiders." This is the great obstacle to evangelism. It doesn't matter how aggressive we are in inviting others to church, or putting up welcome signs out in front; until we learn how to make space for the stranger we will continue to experience the persistent erosion of attendance at worship and a smaller pool of active members.

Hospitality does not mean that everything the community does must include outsiders or the uninitiated. Gentiles could not enter the sanctuary of the Jerusalem Temple; the unbaptized were never included in the fellowship of the Lord's supper. But hospitality does mean that there is an inviting quality to the community's life and worship and that clear signals are given concerning the areas and levels of participation accorded to outsiders or the uninitiated. In our own homes there are certain places and activities which would be out-of-bounds for guests; but certainly the vestibules should be a place where visitors are cordially welcomed and their needs attended to.

Minimally this means that there should be greeters and ushers who say "hello" to strangers, point out facilities they might need, such as rest rooms and nurseries, show them what materials they will need to participate in the liturgy, give some pointers on using the worship book if necessary, and invite them to write their names and addresses in a guest book. There should be a clear statement about participation in holy communion given orally or printed in the worship bulletin. The bulletin should provide useful information about the congregation, such as the address and phone number of the building and the names of the pastor and staff. Bulletin information should be prepared with visitors in mind, since many members of the congregation may also be "visitors" rather than regular participants. Those who prepare announcements should place themselves in the position of visitors or occasional worshipers and ask, "What information do I need to participate intelligently?"

Although the attitudes of those persons stationed in the narthex will do much to establish the sense of the congregation's hospitality, this will also be projected by the architectural design and environment of the congregation's building. Willy Malarcher has described four architectural patterns in the history of Christian liturgy which suggest four models of hospitality.[3]

The ancient Roman house-church, such as the one discovered at Dura-Europos, dating from the third century, suggests a domestic hospitality. Strangers are usually warmly welcomed once they are brought into the family environment, but a private residence, even one deeded over to a community, is not the same as a public place. A certain reserve, even a kind of secrecy, is maintained. This is all the more so in a situation of threatened persecution. But once one has gained admission to the table fellowship, the degree of caring for one another is very great.

There may be a certain romantic nostalgia for the ancient house-church. But it should be recalled that the ancient house-churches could accommodate only a limited number of people—perhaps fifty to sixty if a wall were removed to make a larger place of assembly. The growth of Christianity in the first three centuries was not as dramatic as the opening chapters of the book of Acts might suggest. As far as we know, there were no public orations or mass meetings for evangelistic purposes after the apostolic age. On the contrary, Christians kept a low profile and were wary of strangers. Visitors who were seekers of the faith had to be introduced by members of the Christian community—which is the origin of baptismal sponsorship. And if occasional martyrdoms provided a public advertisement of Christianity, these acts of supreme witness were rarer than has been supposed until the general persecutions which occurred under the emperors Decius and Diocletian. So the setting and hospitality of the house-church provided a counterpart to the actual efforts in evangelism undertaken by the church of the first three centuries. These efforts were low profile and relied to a great extent on personal contact and invitation. Only when the faith was up against the wall of potential apostasy, such as sacrificing to the genius of the emperor, did acts of witness become more overt.

The climate and style of Christian hospitality changed drastically when the church went public in the fourth century and moved into larger public buildings known as basilicas. The Christian basilica paralleled the hospitality of the imperial court, complete with a throne (*cathedra*) from which the bishop could truly preside over the liturgy or public work of the people. Malarcher calls this form of hospitality "monarchical," but it might be more appropriately called "court hospitality." In this model there was a role for everyone in the public assembly. The bishop presided, surrounded by his presbyters, and flanked by his deacons, sub-deacons, acolytes, and other lesser clergy. The faithful filled the central portions of the nave, but there were places on the side for catechumens, in the back for seekers, and on the porch for penitents. This may be a stilted picture of the actual ebb and flow of the crowd in a place with wide aisles in which crowds could be easily accommodated. But the picture is accurate to the extent that everyone gathered in the basilica had an assigned role and knew what was expected of him or her. Above all we should appreciate the *corporate* character of the liturgy celebrated in this kind of place. It was corporate, not in the sense that everyone did the same thing at the same time, but in the sense that everyone had a liturgical role and the whole effect depended on the competent performance of the individual parts.

A shift occurred in the architectural transition from the ancient basilica to the western medieval Romanesque and Gothic church building. The architectural space emphasized the leadership roles of the clergy in the chancel who prayed for and on behalf of the laity gathered in the dimmer recesses of the nave. This arrangement suggested a hierarchical hospitality. One is present at the behest of the priest. This was modified by Baroque architecture in both Roman Catholicism and Protestantism, in which the altar or the pulpit, respectively, dominated the building. But this kind of spatial design still gave a leading role to the clergy who celebrated mass at the altar or preached sermons from the pulpit. This kind of design fostered the perception that people establish a relationship with the minister rather than with the assembly, since the assembly as such was architecturally (and sometimes liturgically) de-emphasized.

Since the Second Vatican Council the concern to draw people into full and active participation in the liturgy has affected church architecture and engendered a relational or circular form of hospitality in which people gather around the Lord's table. In a circle it is difficult to maintain a distinction between insiders and outsiders, or between clergy and laity. This has given vestments a new importance in serving to designate liturgical leadership roles. But the vestments are simplified, just as the environment prompts a reduction in ritual ceremonies, since the space does not lend itself to processions and movement of people; and also in homiletical rhetoric, since there is usually no elevated pulpit from which to deliver an oration. All of this scaling-down may be appreciated by the visitor who is not intimidated by ceremonies or heightened forms of address. On the other hand, there is a loss of a sense of transcendence, of meaning beyond oneself, which may be the very thing the visitor is looking for. The ritual itself must convey a sense of transcendence through recourse to archaism. As the anthropologist Victor Turner observed,

> If ritual is not to be merely a reflection of secular social life, if its function is partly to protect and partly to express truths which make men free from the exigencies of their status incumbencies, free to contemplate and pray as well as to speculate and invent, then its repertoire of liturgical actions should not be limited to a direct reflection of the contemporary scene. Its true modernity should be mediated through forms, some of which, at least, should be inherited. Inherited forms will not be "dead" forms if they have themselves been the product of "free" religious or esthetic creativeness, in brief, of liminality and communitas (between man and God as well as between man and man). Archaic patterns of actions and objects which arose in the past from the free space within liminality can become protective of future free spaces. The archaic is not the obsolete.[4]

How can ritual express the deepest convictions of the faith community and at the same time incorporate the stranger? How can ritual have a pervasively archaic quality which gives to its participants a sense of transcendence, and yet at the same time incorporate those who live in a thoroughly modern world? The closest I have come to experiencing this, outside of certain Christian rituals, is at the weekly Powwow in the Lac du Flambeau, Wisconsin Indian Bowl. Local Native Americans in costume enter the arena and dance around the council ring, with drummers and chanters positioned in the middle of the ring. At various points during the evening spectators are invited to join the dancers in a simple two-step which expresses friendship. (These dances are called "inter-tribal.") Many people come down from their seats to join in the dancing because they are swept up in the events of the evening, and what is expected of them is not all that difficult. But dancing in the bowl gives one a sense of oneness with an alien culture, an identification with its history, as well as providing an expression of fellowship with the present participants.

There are only a few comparable ritual experiences in Christian liturgy. Significantly they occur during holy week when the central mystery of the faith is being celebrated. Examples of rituals which have an archaic but also an inviting quality are: the Palm Sunday procession with palms, coming forward to venerate the cross at the end of the Good Friday liturgy, and gathering around the new fire and processing with a lighted candle into the dark church at the Easter vigil. To some extent, reception of holy communion when the sacrament is administered continuously from a station also gives participants the option of entering into a social activity at their own level of personal intensity and self-consciousness. This is a good example of a ritual which bridges the public and private dimensions of our lives.

There are two models in our society of space which bridge the public and private dimensions of our lives: the public park and the shopping mall. In events which take place in a public park, such as a Fourth of July celebration or a festival such as the Taste of Chicago, everyone gathers for a single purpose—to participate in the event. A sense of community often develops in the celebrative atmosphere (as is also the case in a ball game), but people participate at their own level of interest and intensity. The urban church of antiquity reflected this model since its liturgy often embraced the whole city and a whole day.[5] This is a

99

model which survives, on a reduced scale, in Eastern Orthodox worship (although here the church itself becomes the
world or the public space under the dome of heaven).
There is a sense in Orthodox liturgy of a village gathered to
do its work, with members of the community given the
freedom to participate at their own level of intensity while
coming together to do some things in common (such as
hearing the gospel and receiving communion).

In the shopping mall people also participate in the act
of shopping (the purpose of the mall) at their own level of
interest and intensity. There may be celebrative events going on at certain times or on certain occasions; but these
are at best diversionary and do not focus the attention of
all the people. Therefore, no sense of community or common purpose develops. Indeed, diversity is the goal since
the most successful malls provide the largest number of
attractions for the largest number of people.

It is worth considering that this model has influenced
many suburban churches. Thus, a fifth form of hospitality
can be added to the above-mentioned four: the consumer
hospitality of the shopping mall. Churches have been designed and built with spacious concourses and various
rooms in which are provided a variety of programs and
activities, one of which is the worship space. The drive-
ways and parking lots invite people to enter by providing
easy access to the building and grounds. In this model of
hospitality, what the consumer wants the consumer gets,
and churches bend over backwards to try to be all things to
all people. Within the spectrum of activities offered to the
consumer of religion by modern parishes, worship is one
program among others, even though its importance is tes-
tified to by the fact that the worship room is usually the
largest space in the building. But even worship takes on a
consumer character in the effort to make it as accessible as
possible to the average worshiper. Different kinds of worship experiences may be offered, ranging from "tradi-

tional" to "contemporary." These different services are usually held at different times, but in some fast-growing churches different kinds of worship experiences are offered at the same time in different rooms. The pattern for this was already set by the practice of holding "children's church" at the same time as "adult worship." In this approach, the agonies of trying to be inclusive of different people with different needs within one liturgical assembly is avoided by providing "different strokes for different folks."

The difficulties of pandering to religious consumers hits home for preachers, since one preacher cannot possibly be "all things to all people." In a survey of what members were looking for in a sermon, one affluent suburban congregation came up with this list:

- Need for a pastor who has knowledge of scripture;
- Need for a pastor with theological expertise;
- Need for sermons which have intellectual substance;
- Need to have sermons which are understandable, rather than over people's heads;
- Need to have sermons that speak to our everyday lives and personal needs;
- Need to have sermons which touch the heart and not just appeal to the intellect;
- Need for sermons which are inspirational and spiritually uplifting.

There may be preachers who could fulfill all these expectations, but the average pastor-preacher is not a John Chrysostom, Augustine of Hippo, Martin Luther, or Helmut Thielicke! Diverse expectations of sermons could be met in larger parishes with multiple-staff ministries or by scheduling occasional guest preachers. But somehow lost in all the surveying of church members is the sense that there are preachers so that others may *hear* the word, that the Holy Spirit is somehow involved in the preaching pro-

101

cess, both to inspire the thrust of the sermon and to work faith in those who hear it, and the sense that the humblest proclamation of the word of God may speak a word of gospel or a word of law to me depending on where I stand *coram Deo.*

All this demonstrates what I have referred to elsewhere as "the blessing and bane of celebrating liturgy in our culture."[6] Kenneth Smits points out the twin dangers of "cultural capitulation" and "cultural irrelevancy."[7] We cannot avoid expressing our faith and devotion in forms of expression derived from our own culture, because our culture is a part of our very being. On the other hand, it is a "fallen" reality which can never fully ensconce the gospel without the danger of obscuring the gospel.

The issue of inculturating the liturgy is really the question of authentic celebration and proclamation of the gospel. The address of God in word and sacrament must challenge and liberate those who hear and receive it. This means that the gospel and its liturgical dress must always be adapted to the local worshiping community so that it can be received and understood by the members of the assembly, but without at the same time losing the sense that the church parochial is part of the church catholic. Liturgy and preaching must serve to broaden people's vision of who they are called to be and what their destiny is.

The process of liturgical adaptation to local culture can be seen throughout the history of Christian liturgy, and has even contributed to liturgical development.[8] But the issue can be pushed further than that. G. A. Arbuckle argues that inculturation goes beyond adaptation and raises the issue of indigenization.[9] Adaptation suggests making whatever modifications are necessary as liturgy is translated from one language, culture, doctrinal system, or spirituality into another. Thus, when the Roman liturgy was imported into the Frankish kingdom during the reigns of Pippin and Charlemagne, texts were locally supplied to

102

provide for local observances which were lacking in the Roman books (e.g., the Advent season), or to provide for devotional expressions which would have been foreign to the classical Roman tradition of prayer (e.g., the private, affective prayers said by the celebrant at the offertory and during the communion). Or, in the Lutheran Reformation some texts in the Roman mass which were deemed theologically objectionable were simply deleted (e.g., the offertory prayers and the canon of the mass); and in other instances texts were added to provide for the more overt participation of the people (e.g., the chorales and hymns). But inculturation goes further.

The *Constitution on the Sacred Liturgy* from Vatican II opened up the issue of inculturation by fostering vernacularization. Vernacularization means rooting the liturgy in the language and cultural vitalities of the people who use it. This was an issue Martin Luther clearly saw when he took up the problem of providing a German mass; it could not be just a translation of the Latin texts reset to the old Gregorian chant tunes. A new style of language and a new form of music was needed (e.g., German verse set to chorales). Translating texts from one language to another means probing the forms of expression and accommodating the worldview of the vernacular. The *Pastoral Constitution on the Church in the Modern World* understood this and therefore urged a new appreciation of indigenous cultures. It committed the church to dialogue with the world rather than withdrawing from it. The *Decree on the Missionary Activity of the Church* sees mission flowing from the incarnation of the Word and affirms the continuation of this pattern so that the seeds of the Word (*semina Verbi*) can be planted in every culture. Within the Roman Catholic Church there are only a few instances of inculturation of the liturgy in this sense: the liturgy of Zaire and the liturgies of some Indian churches. It is interesting that inculturation has not occurred more rapidly among Protestant churches than in the Roman Catholic Church in the churches of Africa and Asia, in spite of the fact that Protestants enjoy more freedom to make local changes because of the lack of a central worldwide authority.

The more characteristic Protestant word to describe "inculturation" is "indigenization." One example of this process at work has been the desire to replace Mediterranean or European bread and wine by local food and drink in the eucharist. It springs from the desire to make worshipers feel "at home" in the liturgy and to demonstrate the relevance of the liturgy to everyday life. So it is argued that palm-wine may serve as well as grape-wine to "make glad the heart of man" (Ps 104:15). On the other hand, the historical dimension of the sacrament can be lost unless it is rooted in the specificities of Jesus' institution and the practice of the early church; and there are a wealth of symbolic associations from scripture and tradition favoring the use of bread and grape-wine. We might also note that grape-wine has not always been easily available in some places, such as Scandinavia; yet this did not prompt the desire to use substitutes.

There is thus a fine balance to be maintained between the historic tradition and inculturation or indigenization. This is an issue which needs to be worked out in every local church as worship planners draw upon the gifts, talents, and sensibilities of the members of the local congregation.[10] Sometimes there are overt instances of inculturation or indigenization in congregations serving largely African-American or Hispanic communities in the choice of music, prayer styles, and iconography. In other cases the instances of inculturation or indigenization are more subtle. For example, my present congregation in Evanston, Illinois places a high priority on "scholarly, biblical preaching" and "good music" that undoubtedly reflects the proximity of Northwestern University and the cultural amenities of the Evanston community. This is not a matter of tailoring worship to the outsider or the unchurched, but rather of reflecting the cultural tastes of the members of the congregation. In a natural way, however, others who share the same religious search and are looking for the same kind of edification will be drawn to what has evolved in this parish, as long as the invitation to "come and see" is extended and visitors are hospitably received when they come to look.

This approach represents a conscious decision by the local parish to "specialize." It admits that "we cannot be all things to all people." The advantage of specialization is that it fosters a unified sense of mission and builds up strong bonds of fellowship within the congregation. The congregation has a secure sense of who it is and what it is all about and is able to project this identity and vocation to outsiders and visitors with some degree of enthusiasm.

The danger in this approach is that the church parochial can lose its sense of relatedness to the church catholic, and therefore to the whole mission of God. The members of the local church need to be reminded that while what they do has its own integrity, it is not the only way of worshiping or communicating the gospel. A local church can justify developing a special approach to liturgy and evangelism only if it is conscious of being part of a wider Christian fellowship and mission which, as a whole, is "all things to all people."

There are two ways in which the worship and evangelism of the church parochial can be related to that of the church catholic. In terms of worship, there is the catholic shape of the liturgy; and in terms of evangelism, or mission more broadly considered, there is the apostolic office of the bishop.

The catholic shape of the liturgy can be seen already in the description of Sunday morning worship in Justin Martyr's *First Apology*, chapter 67.[11] By the fourth and fifth centuries there are more ample descriptions of Christian worship in the various church orders. When comparing liturgies representing the East Syrian, West Syrian, Byzantine, Alexandrian, Roman, North African, Milanese, Gallican, Hispanic, and Celtic rites, two factors stand out: first, a variety of cultural expressions are present among the families of rites; and second there is still common to all of them a basic liturgical shape.[12] This shape takes the following order:

> **Entrance rite:** psalmody, litanies, canticles
> **Reading of scripture:** Old Testament, New Testament epistle, gospel—in that order
> **Preaching**
> **Intercessions for all sorts and conditions of people**
> **Greeting of peace** (in all but the Roman rite as a transition from the liturgy of the word to the liturgy of the eucharistic meal)
> **Offertory:** procession with the gifts, psalmody, prayer over the gifts
> **Great Thanksgiving**
> **Communion**
> **Dismissal**

There has been special concern among the so-called "liturgical churches" to relate to the African-American culture. Here we need to differentiate between a common core of religious culture and particular liturgical orders. No group of people, including African-Americans, is monolithic. Nevertheless, it may be possible to identify a common core of African-American religious culture. Elements in this culture may include full sensory participation which comprehends not only dancing and hugging but also colorful vestments, processions, and sometimes "bells and smells;" a sense for "feeling the Spirit" which encour-

106

ages spontaneous prayer and gives emotional license to in-
ject personal needs into the concerns of the community;
up-front musical leadership (instrumentalists and choirs)
which leads the congregation in powerful singing which
draws on musical idioms that are current in the African-
American culture (blues, jazz, spirituals, gospel songs); and
imaginative preaching which blends textual exposition
with justice-oriented applications, vocally supported by
congregational acclamations and exclamations which
makes preaching an antiphonal act. To be sure, these
forms of expression may be found in the free church orders
of worship which are used in Baptist, Methodist, A.M.E.,
and Pentecostal churches which have large black memberships. But there is no reason why a "black style" of worship cannot be observed in an order of worship which follows the catholic shape of the liturgy.[13]

Finding ways to do multicultural liturgy is more prob-
lematic than finding ways to do cultural liturgy. Multicultural liturgy is a conscious attempt to help all members of a
liturgical assembly, regardless of their culture and language, to feel "included" in the celebration. Here we
should note that the historic liturgy of the church is already a multicultural expression in that it retains vestiges
of all the cultures it has passed through (e.g., Semitic,
Greek, Latin, Romance, Germanic, etc.). Lutheran Reformation liturgy was often bi-lingual (Latin, vernacular). It is
not unusual to retain "foreign words" in such a liturgy
(e.g., "Amen",–Hebrew; "Kyrie eleison"–Greek; "Alleluia"–Latinized Hebrew). In some liturgical assemblies
hymns and songs have been used which have foreign language refrains. While it can be asserted that particular
groups have a right to worship regularly using their own
language and cultural expressions, there is still value in
planning multicultural liturgies because such celebrations
evoke a strong sense of catholicity—embracing the whole
people of God in Christ Jesus. Planning such liturgies re-

107

quires a concern to suppress the dominant culture's natural imperialistic proclivities. Attention should be given to environment and art as well as music, the word in proclamation, and the concerns voiced in prayer.[14]

The foregoing reminds us that the feminist movement has raised the question of "inclusive language" in worship. This is an issue properly considered under the headings of "hospitality" and "inculturation." A near consensus has emerged within mainline American churches that we should avoid "false generics" in our speech, such as using "man," "sons," or "brothers/brotherhood," when we are referring to a community which includes both women and men. Efforts at producing "inclusive language lectionaries" have not resulted in nearly such a consensus, although the New Revised Standard Version of the Bible may help in this regard. What readings should be read, or not read, is even more controversial, but it has to be admitted that there is a lack of stories about women in the history of salvation, as disciples of Jesus, or in the early church, in the common lectionary selections. Language used in naming God is most controversial of all. But the debate has forced us to see the variety and plurality of names of God in the Bible, including "I Am who I am" (*Ego eimi*); "Lord" (*Kyrios,* applied to Christ); as well as "Abba" (Father) in the New Testament. Without denying the specific names given to us in the biblical witness, we may still employ a greater selection in our prayer texts and also remember that the given names of God serve to preserve God's mystery as well as reveal God's identity.[15]

Inculturation can take place without obscuring the catholic shape of the liturgy. At the same time the apostolic office of bishop provides for pastoral oversight of various forms and styles of outreach and celebration within one local church. We are rediscovering that to speak of bishops as "successors of the apostles" means that they have a unique responsibility for the apostolic mission of the church.

We have asserted that the mission of the church includes the proclamation of the word and the celebration of the sacraments in the liturgical assembly. From earliest times bishops had primary responsibility for preaching and presiding at the eucharist and Christian initiation.[16] Once the local church reached such a size that the bishop could no longer preside over the whole local assembly, arrangements were made to demonstrate symbolically the unity of the local church in the bishop's eucharist. In the earliest *Ordines Romani*, the bishop presided at different stations in the city of Rome with as many of the clergy and people attending the station mass as possible. Portions of the bread from the bishop's eucharist were sent by acolytes to presbyters or suffragan bishops presiding in other locations. This custom was called the *fermentum*.[17] In Transalpine Europe, where the dioceses were much larger and it was not possible for all the people to attend the bishop's church, the bishop went by horseback to visit local congregations. This is the origin of a rite of confirmation separate from baptism. Because the bishop could not preside at all the baptisms, local presbyters officiated at the water-baptism and first communion but the post-baptismal rite of the imposition of hands and the invocation of the Holy Spirit was deferred until such time as the bishop could be present.[18] This meant that confirmation could be separated from baptism by years. It eventually came to be regarded as an adolescent rite which grants an "increase in grace" to those who have been baptized as infants.

Nevertheless, the practice of confirmation of adolescents will continue because the church needs an adolescent rite of passage even if confirmation remains "a practice seeking a theory."[19] The practice of confirmation by the bishop continues to commend itself because it provides a reason for the bishop to make a systematic visitation of parishes or congregations, and it connects those being confirmed in local parishes or congregations with the wider mission of the church represented by the office of the bishop.

We might recall that the evangelization of Europe over a period of a thousand years from about 400 to 1400 was largely the work of missionary bishops or of episcopal supervision. The names of such bishops as Patrick, apostle to Ireland, Augustine, apostle to England, Willibrord, apostle to the Frisians, Boniface, apostle to the Germans, Ansgar, apostle to the Scandinavians, Cyril and Methodius, apostles to the Slavs, stand out among others. Each of these missionaries either was a bishop or was given episcopal responsibilities as a consequence of his missionary work. In many cases, these missionary bishops were also monks, and one of the essential missionary strategies was to plant communities of word and sacrament in missionary territory.[20]

The bishop today is the person who is in a position to articulate and give leadership to the mission of the territorial church. This is often done through the course of diocesan or synodical administration. But it is also done in the course of episcopal visitations in congregations, parishes, agencies, and institutions. The bishop has an opportunity to preach the word like any other minister of the word and sacraments. But within that context the bishop interprets the mission of the wider church and relates the mission of the local church to the mission of the church catholic. This should be done at every opportunity, whether the bishop's visit is a confirmation, a parish anniversary, the installation of a pastor, or the dedication of a building. At the same time there must be occasions when the bishop needs to make pronouncements not only to the whole territorial church but to the world. These statements, given *ex cathedra*, from the seat of teaching authority, are usually delivered at the bishop's own church, the cathedral. This should be the church in its most public mode: the bishop surrounded by his clergy and the lay leaders of the parishes and congregations, thus showing the collegiality and unity of the church.

We have come a long way in this chapter, and it may seem that disparate elements and ideas have been thrown together. But a summary may help to show the progression of thought that has unfolded in this chapter on "Invitational Evangelism." From the idea of inviting people to church we went on to consider the atmosphere of hospitality that is conveyed by the congregation through its members and facilities. A whole world is being enacted in the liturgy of the church. This is a world with which the visitors must be able to connect. At the same time it must be a world transformed and not just enacted in its fallen condition. The visitor sees the familiar transformed by grace into a new and inviting reality. Worship should project a vision of the new creation which alone can provide hope to those who experience the inadequacies and failures of "this world." Local worship must and will reflect and express local culture. But complete cultural capitulation is avoided by observing the catholic shape of the liturgy and by accepting the leadership of the apostolic office.

When the Public Comes to Church: Festivals and Occasional Services

Every time the doors of a church building are opened, the congregation must be prepared to receive visitors. Practices of hospitality must be intact and attention must be given to liturgical inculturation so that guests will feel welcome and not totally alienated by what is transpiring in the assembly. We have argued that this does not mean tailoring the congregation's liturgy to outsiders. We will argue that an arduous process must be in place to initiate outsiders into the church's liturgical and sacramental life. But there are times when the outside public comes into the church in greater number to attend liturgical events. One thinks of major festivals, such as Christmas and Easter, as well as occasional services, such as baptisms, confirmations, weddings, and funerals. These liturgies put a greater strain on a congregation's practices of hospitality, and it may be that what can be learned from these experiences can have a beneficial impact on the more usual worship services.

First, however, we need an attitude change. In the previous chapter I commented on our reluctance to receive the public. This is sometimes transformed into outright hostility at times of festivals and occasional services. We comment on the lack of regular participation of those whom we see only at Christmas and Easter. We are scandalized by the lack of churchly behavior of those who attend baptisms, confirmations, and weddings. We wonder how a community of strangers can be constituted as a community of faith to send a deceased baptized Christian to the church triumphant. We need to recover the sense that we are all "strangers and pilgrims" both in this world (as Christians) and in the Lord's house (as worshipers). As the author of I Peter put it: "Once you were no people but now you are God's people; once you had not received mercy but now you have received mercy" (2:9).

It is important to attend to the witness, especially in the gospel of Luke, of Jesus as the stranger. A hymn in the *Service Book and Hymnal* of the Lutheran Church in America expressed this better than any hymn I know of in current hymnals.[1]

> Thou didst leave thy throne
> And thy kingly crown
> When thou camest to earth for me,
> But in Bethlehem's home
> Was there found no room
> For thy holy nativity:
> O come to my heart, Lord Jesus;
> There is room in my heart for thee.

Jesus and his family were strangers in Bethlehem in need of hospitality. There was "no room in the inn" and Mary had to give birth in a borrowed stable. Many times later on Jesus would be a guest at someone's table. Since Jesus and his disciples engaged in no sustained labor and had given up regular family life, they had to depend on the hospitality of many, both rich and poor, pillars of society as well as outcasts and sinners.

113

Of course, Jesus is presented as the stranger who becomes the host.[2] This happened already in the nativity story in Luke. The holy family entertained the visiting shepherds. In Luke's description of banquets, Jesus enters the scene as a guest. But as the meal proceeds, the roles of guest and host are reversed. For example, in the house of Simon the Pharisee, Jesus is first presented as the guest. But then Jesus takes charge by telling a story and by announcing God's forgiveness to the woman who anointed his feet. But we note that Jesus is revealed as the ultimate host through the woman, who was also a stranger.

This same reversal occurs after the resurrection. Luke presents a memorable scene on the road to Emmaus. A stranger joins two of Jesus' disciples who are discussing the events that had just happened in Jerusalem. As they walk, this stranger begins to explain to them how the law and the prophets and the psalms pointed to Jesus' ministry and destiny. As they reach their home, he begins to walk on, but the disciples offer him their hospitality and he accepts.

They sit down to eat and the stranger takes the bread, blesses it, and breaks it. In the breaking of the bread—an act of hospitality—the stranger is revealed to them as the risen Lord.

The relationship of host and guest takes on an ultimate claim in the parable of the last judgment in Matthew 25:31ff. Jesus appears as the Son of man who comes in glory and begins dividing the righteous from the unrighteous. To the righteous he talks about how they provided for him; to the unrighteous he says, "I was a stranger and you did not welcome me. . . ." When the unrighteous ask when it was that they failed to provide hospitality to Jesus, he replies: "Truly, I say to you, as you did it not to one of the least of these, you did it not to me."

Matthew concludes: "And they will go away into eternal punishment, but the righteous into eternal life."

To those gathered in Roman house-churches, the apostle Paul wrote: "Welcome one another, therefore, as Christ welcomed you, for the glory of God" (Rom 12:13). This was a summary of one of the situations Paul addressed in Corinth. He had written to the Corinthians that they should not confuse their own private meals with the Lord's supper, and therefore they had to wait for one another (I Cor 11:17ff.). Even if the eucharist was celebrated in a private home, which was probably the case, and even though the owner was used to playing host and providing hospitality to his guests, which was the likely situation, the owner of the house was not the host when the church met for the Lord's supper; Christ was. The supper was to proclaim Christ.[3]

Even if the congregation or the diocese holds title to the church building, God's word is proclaimed and Christ's sacraments are celebrated within it. The church built the place but invited Christ in. Christ came in as guest but took over as host. That puts all the worshipers into the same category: they are guests of Christ. This should inform our understanding of congregational hospitality.[4]

With this in mind let us look at our practices of hospitality at special liturgical events such as major festivals and occasional services. We will reflect on who the "outsiders" might be at such times, how their presence might shape our celebrations, and how the preacher's awareness of their presence might influence the content of the sermon.

Most churches experience large crowds for the festivals of Christmas and Easter because these liturgical days enjoy cultural support in our North American social context. Included in these crowds are people who are not "outsiders" in the formal sense since they are members of the congregation. But their church participation is perhaps so irregular during the rest of the year that they are "strangers" to the congregation's ways of doing things. Also included among the strangers are relatives of members who have come together because of the holidays: grandparents, parents, children, grandchildren—perhaps many of them members or former members of the parish who now live most of the year in some other community. Thus, we are not talking about vast numbers of un-churched in the formal sense who fill the ranks of our wor-shiping assemblies on Christmas and Easter, but members, inactive members, nominal members, or former members of the parish—all people with whom the congregation has had a relationship. Nevertheless, if we can plan and con-duct worship on these festival occasions in ways which maintain the lines of communication between the gath-ered congregation and the outsiders and by those outside the gathered congregation to those within, we will have acquired learnings that will hold us in good stead on those occasions when first-time visitors are present.

We need to remember that our liturgical routines are constantly undergoing revision and those who are in-volved week after week are clued in to the evolving prac-tices. But those who have not been in the parish church since last Christmas or Easter are "strangers" to practices that have been developed over the course of the year. So worship leaders need to treat the actual congregation gath-ered for these major festivals as a company of strangers. This does not mean that the celebration should be turned into a classroom experience but that what is done should enable the people to participate easily. The order of service should be clear and, nowadays, with the aid of word proces-sors and desk top publishing, the order can be printed out in the worship folder so that people don't have to bypass options in the worship books. (When extra seating has to be set up to accommodate worshipers there often are not enough worship books to go around anyway.) Familiar hymns and liturgical music should be used on these days. One wonders if this kind of historical experience does not lie behind Anton Baumstark's liturgical law about the tenacity of archaic practices on the solemn days in the liturgical year.[5] In other words, rituals tend to change very little from one year to the next on the most sacred days in the calendar. In part this is because worship leaders have to rely on what they have done before in order to get through tightly-packed days and seasons. But also it reflects the fact that people expect and look forward to certain practices on certain days. There is the nostalgic pull of local traditions which many pastors have discovered sometimes are at odds with the tradition of the church catholic.[6]

This is probably more the case with Christmas Eve than with Easter morning. On Christmas Eve there is an expectation of familiar carols and candlelight. At the same time, Christmas is the "Christ mass," and the word and eucharist should be intact. In some parishes a children's or family service has become popular at an early hour in the evening. Often the children enact the Christmas gospel in a pageant. Even so, the pastor would be remiss not to have a homily and to offer communion. Parents who attend such a service are unlikely to be able to return for a later service of word and sacrament. The homily at such a service might be geared toward children, and a eucharistic prayer from masses with children might be used. But adults will not necessarily feel excluded by this kind of fare, whereas on most occasions children are totally excluded by words that are beyond them.

The Christmas gospel, of course, is an inexhaustible source of homiletical inspiration. The nativity story in Luke 2 addresses the human situation in so many ways.

Luke sets it within human history. There are complications for Mary and Joseph arising from a governmental requirement. There is the issue of housing and human compassion for a young couple in need. There is the fact that the angelic announcement was made to the most unlikely candidates for divine revelation. There is the heavenly celebration with most of the earth apparently unaware of it. There is the utter condescension of the divine into the humblest human conditions. The sample sermon provided here picks up the idea of the shepherds as evangelists and the response to their testimony. People were simply "amazed."

SERMON FOR CHRISTMAS EVE
TEXT: LUKE 2:1–20

Christmas is a time for story-telling. There is probably no other time of the year for which there are more stories to be told or to be seen on television. And probably no story is more frequently told, or more greatly loved, than the story we have heard read (and enacted) tonight: St. Luke's story about the birth of Jesus and the announcement of this to shepherds by an angel of the Lord. Matthew had a story about Jesus' birth too: the story of wise men who saw a strange star in the sky and followed it to where there was a baby whom they worshiped as the messiah of the Jews. Sometimes, in our crèche scenes and Christmas pageants, we join these two stories together. But its really best to keep them separate, because they have different messages for us. On the feast of the Epiphany we will hear the story of the wise men. Tonight we want to think about the story of the shepherds.

Its the story of a man and a woman who have to return to their hometown due to some government regulation, and when they arrive the woman—a young girl, really—is ready to have a baby. They need hospitality, but do not receive it. The inns were full. The best someone could do was to let them set up housekeeping in a stable, where their baby was born. This will become a recurring theme in Luke's gospel. Jesus is the stranger who needs hospitality. But when it is provided, he takes over and becomes the host.

That happened even the night he was born. He and his family played host to some shepherds. Now shepherds are interesting people. Some of Israel's greatest leaders had been shepherds: Abraham and Moses and David. But we shouldn't glamorize the shepherds. They led a rough life and they could be crude men. They were important to society, because they raised what was eaten and worn. But the townspeople would be just as happy if the shepherds stayed out in the hills with their sheep because they could be pretty rowdy when they came into town. Whenever something was stolen, people blamed the shepherds.

But the shepherds came to town the night Jesus was born—not because the townspeople invited them or even wanted them to come—but because the angel of the Lord told them to go to see what God had done.

And what had God done? Had he performed some great extravagant feat that would blow you away with its awesomeness? No, he simply arranged for a baby to be born. The great gift of God—a long-awaited savior —was wrapped in diapers and laid in a manger. God does not overpower us with his gifts. There was no extravaganza of presents lying around a Christmas tree. Just a baby lying in a manger or in the lap of his young mother. How gentle God is in the way he deals with us!

And when the shepherds saw God's gift, they told others about it. But the story says, "all who heard it were amazed at what the shepherds told them." It doesn't say that they believed the shepherds; just that they were amazed. It's probably the interpretation that amazed them. It's not so amazing that a young couple would have a baby. That's what young couples have. And babies have been born in all kinds of makeshift arrangements. But that God was acting through this birth and its peculiar arrangements—that's what was so amazing. I'm inclined to think that people didn't accept the shepherds' interpretation.

We proclaim the message, the word of God, and some people receive it as good news and some people are indifferent to it. What makes the difference? What kind of person hears the message and receives it as good news? Certainly most people do not. People who are receptive to good news are people who *need* to have good news; but more than that, they are people who *want* to hear good news. Their hearts and minds are prepared so that they are *receptive*. The logic of the church's Advent season is to help us prepare our hearts and minds to be receptive to the Christmas gospel. But if we are not receptive, no amount of forced preparation and celebration can help us see this gospel as good news for us, and as something we can respond to with joy.

Many of us, and many people we know, have grown up hearing the announcement of the angels to the shepherds: "To you is born . . . a Savior, Christ the Lord." For many people the message is received along with thousands of other pieces of news. It may be perceived as "good news"—not anything bad that could harm people. But it is not responded to with joy—because such people don't think it makes any difference in their lives. We used to devote a lot of thinking to how we could make this message appeal to or be relevant to the so-called "man in the street." Today the same challenge is before us to be evangelists to the so-called "couch potato," the kind of person who does his or her job and then comes home and doesn't really get too involved with the outside world.

I'm not sure that we can make this announcement appealing to or relevant to such people. The angels didn't go to everybody either. They didn't go to the innkeepers, or other businessmen who were probably busy at that time of the year tending to and making profits from the many people traveling around to go to ancestral homelands for a census enrollment. These people, as far as we know, were not included in what was going on out in the cattle stall. Certainly Matthew's account of Herod's political maneuverings gives no glory to kings.

No, God proved Mary's song correct: he exalted the humble once again. God came among the poor. God's Son was born among the homeless.

Now there's a danger in romanticizing the humble, the poor, the homeless—especially if you've never been that yourself. Nor should we think that God wants the poor to be poor or the homeless to be homeless. But God frequently speaks to us through the voices of those with nothing to lose. They exist at the line of marginal survival; so they have a sense of what constitutes life's essence.

And so the angels announced the divine birth, and the beginning of a new age of peace and justice, to shepherds—humble and crude men who were often looked down on by other people in society. By this act we know that God did not enter the world only for the privileged and the wise, but for common, ordinary people—maybe people like ourselves. By his coming among the lowly, we can know with greater certainty that God's message is for everyone.

If we get an inkling that God's salvation is for everyone, then we can know that it is also for us, whose physical needs may not be very great, but who often have other deep and buried needs. And if we can know that God's salvation is intended also for us, we may, with a tinge of joy or even giddiness, want to tell others about what God has done, even if people are amazed at what we are saying. For the joy of what God has done in the birth of this baby cannot be contained. Joy can never be contained; it always spills over. As the angel said, "I am bringing you good news of great joy for *all*

121

the people." The people must be told. They must be invited to open their hearts to let in this divine stranger who will take over and become the host. For that is how Christ comes into our world and advances through it.

> O holy Child of Bethlehem,
> Descend to us, we pray;
> Cast out our sin, and enter in,
> Be born in us today.

There are other occasions when the outside public is actually invited into the liturgical assembly for special programs or recognitions. These may include a service with a special musical presentation, a celebration of a community program which enjoys and requires cooperative effort on the part of several churches and organizations, or the recognition of a particular community organization, such as Scouting.

In these cases it is not necessary to turn the congregation's normal worship inside out, but it is necessary to provide help to the visitors so that they can participate to the extent they desire. In churches which use worship books, an announcement should be made about where things can be located in the book. Lutherans and Methodists, for example, need to point out that page references to the liturgy are in the front of the book and hymn numbers are in the back of the book. Episcopalians need to point out that two books are needed: the Prayer Book and the Hymnal. Roman Catholics need to alert visitors to what books are being used since there may be an assortment of them in the pews. A clear statement should be made about eucharistic hospitality and how communion is ministered (walking, standing, kneeling, sitting, continuously, by table, in the hand, taking the cup, intincting, picking up an individual glass, etc.). A larger group of ushers should be on hand to help with a larger crowd and members of the congregation should be prepared to help visitors find their way through the service and through the building. On a Sunday when many visitors are expected it might be good to have greeters designated as such stationed at every door to answer questions and to be of assistance.

The sermon on such an occasion should not ignore the specific event which brought outsiders into the church. Nor should it ignore the fact that this is the regular gathering of the congregation for word (and sacrament). In liturgical churches the assigned readings from the lectionary will be read and should receive comment in the sermon. How to bridge these two events—e.g., a community activity and the liturgical day—without doing disservice to either requires homiletical imagination. A sample sermon is provided from February 2, 1992 when Scout Sunday was observed on the festival of the Presentation of Jesus and the Purification of Mary. This combined celebration actually worked out very well and the "youth" emphasis in the service received further support with the recognition of acolytes at the offertory when, in keeping with an old custom of this day, the church's supply of candles for the year was blessed (hence the name "Candlemas"). The religious component of Scouting and the observance of certain rituals on this day correlated well with the devotional practices of the holy family in the gospel for the Presentation. There is no guarantee that seemingly disparate elements would have come together so well on, say, the Fourth Sunday after the Epiphany. We chose February 2 as Scout Sunday because we saw these possibilities. The lesson here is that worship planners should pay attention to the liturgical possibilities when planning these kinds of celebrations. The feast of the Presentation will not be a possibility again until 1998, when it again falls on a Sunday. But the sample sermon is included here also for the way it advances the argument of this book.

SERMON FOR THE FEAST OF THE PRESENTATION
TEXT: LUKE 2:22–40

Turtledoves and pigeons—that's what Mary and Joseph had to offer in order for Mary to be purified after childbirth and for Jesus to be "redeemed" from being taken by God. For as the firstborn male, Jesus had to be presented—actually offered—to God. But the sacrifice of a year-old lamb in thanksgiving and a turtledove as a sin offering served to "redeem" Jesus from being taken by God and to purify Mary for giving birth. Actually, since they were poor, in place of the lamb they could offer a pair of turtledoves or two young pigeons.

From our theological standpoint, there seems to be something almost blasphemous about the pure Mother having to be purified for having given birth to the Son of God, and the Son of God having to be redeemed from God's use. Also, from our standpoint as modern Gentiles, there is something scandalous about the whole notion of purification and presentation. But it made sense to the ancient Jews that a woman is drained of vitality in childbirth and must be ritually restored to the source of life—God himself. It also made sense that everything in life is a gift from God and should therefore be received with thanksgiving. We still believe that it is appropriate to show a token of appreciation for a favor received, and that's what pious Jews did by offering the sacrifice of thanksgiving.

Mary and Joseph too "performed everything according to the law of the Lord." Luke tells us that they had Jesus circumcised when he was eight days old. Forty days after childbirth Mary went through the rites of purification and Jesus was presented to God in a sacrifice of thanksgiving. Later, at the age of twelve,

Jesus was again in the Temple. Luke tells us that Jesus' parents went to Jerusalem "every year at the Feast of the Passover," but the Passover of Jesus' twelfth year was especially important because it was part of the preparation for his bar mitzvah at age thirteen.

These are the only stories we have about the childhood of Jesus, and it is noteworthy that Luke is the only evangelist who reports them. It is noteworthy because Luke was not a Jew and he was presumably writing to a Greco-Roman audience. What interest would Gentiles have in such things? A lot! Greeks and Romans were very interested in ancient and, for them, somewhat exotic religious practices. Romans in particular were very concerned to follow prescribed rituals in their own civil religion. Far from being scandalized, Luke's Greco-Roman readers would have been impressed by this record of painstaking devotion to hallowed Jewish traditions.

Later on, it would seem that Jesus was not in agreement with the contemporary leaders of Israel about the purposes of these traditions. From Mark's gospel one gets the impression that Jesus was ready to abolish these practices. In Matthew's gospel it seems that Jesus was probing the roots of these traditions to observe them with the integrity called for by the prophets. In John's gospel it is clearly the case that Jesus replaces these traditions with himself. But in Luke's gospel there is the sense that Jesus humanizes these practices. There does not seem to be the polemic against the rites and sacrifices that one finds, for example, in Mark. And this leads to two thoughts.

One is that no matter where we end up, there is value in giving our children a sound religious upbringing by observing the customs and rituals of the faith community. The Boy Scouts of America support this point of view in a very interesting way which takes into account the religious pluralism of our society. The Scout oath includes a promise to do one's duty "to God and my country." The 12th Scout law is reverence. The

125

wolf and bear badges in cub scouts include performing a service to one's religious community and discussing one's religious duty with one's family members. A religious upbringing is taken seriously and the values that come from that upbringing are reinforced, but without endorsing any set of religious beliefs and practices. There is even room for those with no particular affiliation with a religious institution or community, as long as there is the recognition of some ultimate claims on human life which are codified by the symbolic word "God" and a sense of reverence. To my mind Scouting offers a model which would provide a way out of the muddled mess that has surrounded religion in public life in America in recent years. There are ways for a pluralistic society to take religion seriously without forcing any one religion on others.

The other thought is that it is precisely through these ritual traditions that we encounter what is truly human. God doesn't need our rituals, but *we* need them. We need them because whether they are the macro-rituals of religious tradition which deal with issues of life and death, or the micro-rituals of family life or den meetings, they enable us to express what is important to us: our meanings and values. Show me any group of people who have lost the ability to communicate through meaningful ritual action, and I'll show you a society that is disintegrating. As the psychologist Erik Erikson wrote, "the decay or perversion of ritual does not create an indifferent emptiness, but a void with explosive possibilities." "Perhaps," he went on to say, this "explains why 'nice' people who have lost the gift of imparting values by meaningful ritualization can have children who become (or behave like) juvenile delinquents; and why nice 'churchgoing' nations can so act as to arouse the impression of harboring pervasive murderous intent."

Luke means to tell us that God works through such human means as rituals and traditions. And the Jesus we meet in this gospel is a real human being. Our reading today ends with the notation that Jesus grew and became strong. He ran and played. He did chores around the house and probably bothered Joseph in his carpenter's shop. He undoubtedly received the kind of education any Jewish boy would have received. Jews had to be literate because they had to be able to read the scriptures. I have no doubt that if Jesus were among us today, he would probably join Boy Scouts, go camping, take piano lessons, and play soccer on Saturday mornings.

Sometimes the humanity of Christ offends us. We have so overemphasized his divinity! We are accustomed to pictures of Jesus with a beatific look on his face, surrounded by a halo, gazing into the eternal distance, that we find it difficult to imagine how he could be like us. Today's epistle reminds us, however, that in order to save us Jesus "had to become like his brothers and sisters in every respect, so that he might be a merciful and faithful high priest in the service of God, to make a sacrifice of atonement for the sins of the people. Because he himself was tested by what he suffered, he is able to help those who are being tested." Only someone who knows what we are experiencing is able to provide the help we need. As Dietrich Bonhoeffer wrote from his prison cell in Nazi Germany, "Only a suffering God can help."

When old Simeon held Jesus in his arms, he was not looking at the face of a god but at the face of a baby. Yet both he and aged Anna recognized in this child God's saving intentions and gave thanks. But God's salvation was not a plan; it was a person. And while God's salvation was meant for everyone—Jews and Gentiles alike—not all would accept it. The child, said Simeon, was to be "a sign that would be opposed." And Mary would be a "sorrowing mother," as her name itself indicated.

Jesus forced himself on no one. And it would be wrong for the church to force its Lord on anyone. But to those who receive him he brings a way of dealing

127

with our present maladies and gives the sure hope of a
future in the "joy and peace" of God. And the church is
surely right to invite people to discover this for themselves. Amen.

There are times when large numbers of strangers come
into the worship space for occasional services that deal
with what anthropologists and historians of religion call
"the sanctification of life": baptisms, confirmations, weddings, and funerals. Most baptisms and confirmations in
Protestant churches take place in a Sunday service of the
congregation and most of the outsiders are guests of
church members. Concern might be given to making sure
that church members can help their guests through the
service. But for weddings and funerals there are the possibilities that outsiders will outnumber the members of the
congregation in attendance.

A wedding service is usually planned over a period of
months with the bride and groom. Planning will include
such considerations as who the guests will be and the level
of their ability to participate in the service. This will gov-
ern such decisions as whether hymns or other pieces of
liturgical music will be sung, if so which ones, whether
holy communion will be celebrated, and how it will be
ministered. At the wedding rehearsal there are usually family members in attendance in addition to those who are in
the actual wedding party. The presiding minister should
take the opportunity to go through the whole service,
coaching all the participants in their responses.

A marriage service is a service of the church. To whatever extent possible, members of the church should be present to extend hospitality and to assist in the celebration.
Christian marriage is celebrated under the word of God
and the service should include both reading and proclamation of the word. The homily may be directed specifically
to the bride and groom, but all who hear it have an occa-

sion to reflect on their own marriage in the light of the word. The sample homily included here was given at the wedding of two graduate students involved in linguistic and cultural studies. Only one of the couple had any church background; the other was unchurched. The couple selected the readings for the marriage service during planning sessions with the pastor. The background of the couple and the somewhat unusual selection of readings presented a homiletical challenge, complicated by the fact that wedding homilies need to be succinct. For better or for worse it is included here as a sample of a homily that must be apologetic because of the number of non-church persons in attendance, but also articulate the church's hope for the restoration of all things—including marriage—in God's kingdom.

THE WEDDING OF JANE AND KEITH
TEXTS: TOBIT 8:4-9; PSALM 121; ROMANS 12:1-2; JOHN 15:9-12

Jane and Keith, in their careers as scholars, have an interest in cultures, with their customs and rituals. They are immersed profoundly in the customs and rituals of their own culture today. Keith and Jane: this is for real, and it is both dangerous and difficult. From an anthropological point of view, we could say that you are going through a ritual of passage with this wedding ceremony that gives you public permission to make love and has, as its consequence, the making of relatives. That's why it's both dangerous and difficult. It's dangerous because the powerful things that marriage makes—love and relatives—can be unmade. It's difficult because those things we make up, like our fictions and our weddings, also make us up and may even outlive us. We cannot always unmake what we have made just by deciding to do so. You are tapping into something outside yourselves today—call it a "force" or an "institution" (the terms are inadequate)—but this "something" does not go away just because warm feelings wane and couples experience conflict.

You have deliberately chosen to demonstrate that you are tapping into this "something" by celebrating your marriage in the context of a worship event. Like the psalmist of ancient Israel, you look to the hills for help, the mountains suggesting the durability and strength of the Lord who watches over his people. Indeed, the Lord does not "slumber" in the seasonal weaknesses of the nature deities whose power is sometimes dormant. But the Lord undertakes to guard constantly and eternally over the life of his people. "Shade" here is virtually a title for the protecting God who covers us in the heat of the day and wards off the ills which the ancients attributed to moonstroke. This is a God who is involved in the lives of people, who watches over our comings and goings, our decisions and our undertakings, for they involve those cultural forces and institutions which are of his design.

There is the force of love and the institution of marriage which you embrace and undertake today— both created by God. Tobias, in our first reading, blesses God for graciously providing that two people can become one flesh through sexual union and provide help and support for each other in the affairs of life.

But we're talking about two individuals with their unique personalities, likes and dislikes, being joined together; and mergers don't happen easily. What St. Paul says about the necessity for life in Christian community also applies to marriage: there must be a giving, a sacrifice, of selves—for this is what is "good and acceptable and perfect" in the mind of God, as that has been disclosed to us in Jesus Christ.

This is not something we will readily or easily do. Such a good and acceptable and perfect expression of love is possible only within the context of Christ's love for us. The new commandment to "love one another" can be fulfilled only because "I have loved you; (so) abide in my love."

This gift of love is what alone can "save" marriage from its dangers and difficulties. We sometimes forget that marriage is, like everything else in culture, fallen and distorted, and that it needs not just to be blessed and solemnized—by the church's functionaries and with the help of the photographer—but *restored.* And this restoration can only take place in the new life in God's kingdom. That is what we tap into today in this worship event, this service or liturgy of marriage, praying that it may be a holy matrimony—a marriage rooted in God, in God's blessing, and in God's saving power. Amen.

Most deaths of church members will involve either a funeral or a memorial service. Funeral services may be held in the church or in a funeral home. Pastors prefer to have the service in the church because of the opportunities for congregational singing and ritual actions. It is possible, but more difficult, to have spirited singing in the muted environment of the funeral home, often with only a small electronic organ to provide accompaniment. The celebration of the eucharistic meal is almost precluded in a funeral home (although I did it once, using a card table and a box of supplies I carried from the sacristy, when a sudden snowstorm made transportation of the body impossible).

Once again, many guests will be participating in the service who may come from other churches or no church at all. The kind of advance planning done for weddings is not possible for funerals. Pastors have to exercize almost instantaneous judgment in terms of what kind of congregation will be in attendance and what the general level of ritual competence will be. Will singing be possible? Will the congregation know how to respond to prayers? With both weddings and funerals, it can be a very depressing experience to expect a company of strangers to respond

131

with the same spontaneity as the Sunday morning congregation.

On the other hand, this is a service of the church. Members of the church should make an effort to attend to give support to those who mourn. This is also a time for the proclamation of the gospel both on behalf of the deceased and to the mourners. The proclamation of the gospel on behalf of the deceased lies in the fact that the Christian funeral does not begin with the physical death of the person, but with spiritual death at the baptismal font. The promises of God made at baptism must be claimed now. Those who hear the commendation of the faithful departed will hear an unambiguous application of the gospel of justification by grace through faith for Christ's sake:

> Into your hands, O merciful Savior, we commend your servant N. Acknowledge, we humbly beseech you, a sheep of your own fold, a lamb of your own flock, a sinner of your own redeeming. Receive him/her into the arms of your mercy, into the blessed rest of everlasting peace, and into the glorious company of the saints in light.[7]

The congregation, even if it is a company of strangers, should be given an opportunity to respond verbally to the prayers of intercession and to give voice to the confession of faith. By participating in this way the faith of the mourners can be awakened and strengthened. Worship can have a reflexive effect. By reciting the creed and the Lord's Prayer when spirits are low, hope can be rekindled. We cannot guarantee that this will always happen, of course, but we need to remember that prayer intends to have as much effect on the pray-er as it does on God. This is why in each of the petitions of the Lord's Prayer Luther, in his Catechism, points out that it is not by our prayers that God's name is hallowed, God's kingdom comes, or God's will is done, etc; but we pray that God's name will be hallowed by us, that God's kingdom will include us, that God's will may be done by us, etc.[8]

It would be a mistake in a funeral or any service to leave the congregation mute because they are a company of strangers. In uttering responses and making statements a person moves from one stance to another and risks a new relationship with God and others. Such a person becomes liable to a commitment that may not have been there before. Far from being seen as a threat, such declarative expressions may actually be welcomed by many worshipers. The human need to assert the self is a fundamental drive. But most of us live pathetically bottled up and lack the opportunities to express ourselves. Rituals provide us with these opportunities. They are opportunities to express ourselves even in public in ways we would not dare to do in private. Such ritual occasions are intrinsically satisfying and are generally appreciated by those who are invited to participate in them. It would be a missed opportunity, sometimes of tragic proportions, for the church to fail to provide people with ways of expressing their deepest thoughts and feelings simply because of a failure of nerve over a fear that "people won't respond."

Liturgy and Evangelism: Calendar Coordination

We began with a discussion of the uncertain relationship between liturgy and evangelism. We have argued that liturgy is an evangelistic activity because it is a proclamation and celebration of the gospel. Worship in word and sacraments is an integral part of God's mission of reconciling the world to himself because the acts of proclamation of the gospel and administration of the sacraments are the very means of grace by which God calls, gathers, enlightens, and sanctifies a people who shall be "a light to the nations." It is appropriate to invite people to come to church—to where the word is preached and the sacraments administered—because that is an arena of encounter between God and humanity. In this arena they meet Jesus who shows us the God who is his Father. Because we are inviting people to "come and see" we must attend to our hospitality to strangers and visitors and the inculturation of the gospel in ways that make it accessible to and connected with the local culture. In short, we must attend to the whole climate of evangelism in the congregation. There is nothing a congregation does that does not have some impact on its public presentation, from its ways of incorporating visitors and strangers in its patterns of fellowship to the upkeep of its buildings and grounds. But

134

finally we want to say that a liturgical church, that is, a church which lives from its liturgy, must develop a liturgical evangelism. A model for this can be found in the initiation practices of ancient Christianity. Indeed, the rites of Christian initiation made all-consuming demands on the church's time and energy and influenced the development of the church year. Liturgy serves evangelism as the ritual means of bringing converts to new birth in Christ and incorporating those newly-born in Christ into the body of Christ in the world—the church.

It would be good for pastors and lay people to become acquainted with the practices of Christian initiation in the ancient church as these practices are known to us from the texts of church orders, homilies, and sacramentaries. In particular, *The Apostolic Tradition* of Hippolytus of Rome,[1] the mystagogical homilies of the leading bishops of the time,[2] and the texts of the Gelasian Sacramentary related to holy baptism[3] are recommended as pivotal in understanding the development of the "awe-inspiring rites of initiation," as they were sometimes called.

Apart from helping us to understand the background of Lent and holy week, studying these texts is important because they provide us with a model for Christian initiation which is relevant to the church's current needs for "making Christians." The rites developed before the church became an official, or even a legal, religion, and the church today exists in a "post-Christian" society in the western world. In fact, at the time of Hippolytus, Christians were a persecuted minority and Hippolytus himself ended his life as a martyr in the salt mines of Sardinia. In this situation there was a clear need for the extensive guidance and instruction of converts, just as today we cannot assume that non-church members have a reliable understanding of Christianity or what the Christian life entails. At the time of Hippolytus there was a need to lure people away from pagan spiritualities and sensibilities through the process of conversion, just as today the influence of secularism must be countered if the church is to produce real disciples of Jesus. There is no point in reinventing the wheel. These ancient orders can serve as models for our own efforts in evangelization.

As a greater portion of the population became Christian, infant baptism became more prevalent. We need not go into the reasons for this development here.[4] It is sufficient to note that this was the case by the early Middle Ages in both the eastern and western Churches. It may be further noted that Christian influences within society as a whole could be counted on to help make Christians. This was the situation in the age of Christendom and its Christian culture, which lasted for well over a thousand years in Europe. The advent of humanism at the time of the Renaissance formed cracks in the culture of Christendom, but the advent of secularism in the Age of Revolution fractured the culture of Christendom. Albert Camus suggested that the decapitation of the French king was synonymous with the death of God that Friedrich Nietzsche was later to proclaim. The whole "death of God" movement of a generation ago attempted to serve notice of a cultural incapacity for God. The consequences of this are evident in those places in Europe and North America where vast portions of the population are Christian in name only, and generations of unbaptized persons are to be found in urban centers living in the shadows of church spires.

In North America Christianity may still be the largest religion, but other religions are growing quickly. These include Islam, Buddhism, and Hinduism, along with the Jewish presence that has always existed alongside the Christian. A large portion of the population is non-religious and the official stance of the state is to be religiously neutral. So we cannot expect the schools, the media, and the arts to help infuse a Christian worldview and value system into society as was the case in the culture of

Christendom. What it takes to make Christians, the church must do on its own.

In this situation, conversion is going to have to play a more important role than was previously the case in the practices of mainline denominations. Conversion means "change." It requires that we move beyond where we are and where we feel comfortable to a new stance and a new way of being that God calls us to be. The church is going to have to help people change the orientation of their lives and how to translate new meanings into new modes of behavior. This is why there is so much discussion about a "return to the catechumenate" or the development of a "life-long catechumenate." We have to take seriously once again the statement of Tertullian that "Christians are made, not born."

The Roman Catholic Church recognized the reality of this situation when the Sacred Congregation for Divine Worship published the Rite of Christian Initiation for Adults (R.C.I.A.) in 1972.[5] The rite recovers the sacramental economy of the ancient church in its linkage of baptism and first communion. But it also recovers the ancient church's ritual process for "making Christians." It takes seriously the arduous task of honing the embryonic faith of those who seek "the living God" by channeling it into a community of faith where it may be given articulation and engaged in a life of service and witness. The full rite is done in four stages over a long period of time:

First Stage: Rite of Becoming Catechumens
   I. Introductory Rite
  II. Celebration of the Word of God
 III. Catechumenate and Its Rites (exorcism, blessing, anointing)

Second Stage: Rite of Election or Enrollment of Names
  I. Presentation of the Candidates
 II. Examination of Candidates

137

   III. Admission or Election
   IV. Celebration of the Eucharist (but only "after the elect leave")
    V. Period of Purification and Enlightenment or Illumination (three masses of the scrutinies, presentations of the Creed and Lord's Prayer, profession of faith, rite of opening ears and mouth)

Third Stage: Celebration of the Sacraments of Initiation
     I. Celebration of Baptism
    II. Explanatory Rites (anointing, clothing, lighted candle)
   III. Celebration of Confirmation
   IV. Celebration of the Eucharist (first communion)
    V. The Period of Post-Baptismal Catechesis or Mystagogia

There are, within this scheme, really four different but continuous periods, each marked by major and minor ritual transitions:[6]

- the precatechumenate
- the catechumenate
- the period of purification and enlightenment or illumination
- the post-baptismal catechesis or mystagogy.

The precatechumenate is the time when "seekers" respond to the church's invitation to "come and see." It is marked by formal and informal contacts and conversation with pastors and laity about what Christianity is, what the church is, and why Christians do or don't do certain things. From these "curiosity seekers" emerge candidates who are ready to embrace the church's faith. These persons are enrolled into the catechumenate.

The catechumenate is marked by more intense doctrinal instruction, Bible study, engagement in acts of ministry, and a series of rites in which false worship and occult practices are renounced and the blessing of God is invoked. In the catechumenal rites exorcisms of unclean spirits are balanced with the anointings of the Holy Spirit.

The period of purification and enlightenment is the intense time of catechesis during Lent in which catechumens are scrutinized, declared "elect," and presented with items of the faith such as the Apostles' and Nicene Creeds and the Lord's Prayer. (We note that in the ancient sacramentaries, the elect were also presented with the four gospels.)

The final phase includes the celebration of the "sacraments of initiation"—baptism, confirmation, and first communion—at the Easter vigil. But the process continues for the seven weeks after Easter day—the period of mystagogia—when the neophytes are given further instruction on the sacraments they have just experienced.

This process of education and ritual addresses the problem of the gap between the life of the church and the knowledge and values of the unchurched. Rather than turning the church inside out to meet the unchurched "where they are," the unchurched are initiated by careful steps into the fullness of the church's life. The scope of this process is such that it cannot be just one program among others. It resists any kind of "quick fix" approach to evangelism. If Christian initiation is done right, it requires all of the church's time, talents, and energy, as reflections on the experience of the R.C.I.A. indicates.[7] R.C.I.A. requires the active participation of the whole congregation. Lay persons as well as clergy serve as catechists, sponsors and godparents. The whole leadership of the local church cannot be employed in this kind of extensive process without the process itself having an impact on the identity and mission of the community. As Aidan Kavanagh commented:

> The importance of the restored rites of adult initiation lies therefore less in its ceremonial details than in its strategic vision of the Church local and universal. It is a practicable vision of what the Church is and can become through the continuing renewal process of evangelization, conversion, catechesis, and the paschal sacraments of Christian initiation.[8]

As important as this rite is for helping us to rethink our practices of evangelism and initiation, we also have to realize that among the vast numbers of the unchurched in our society are baptized Christians who are no longer actively involved in the life and mission of the church. There are, for example, those who drifted away from church attendance after confirmation or when they left home to go to college or military service or just to be on their own. The population explosion which produced the "baby boomers" indicates that there are many young and middle-aged inactive Christians among us. These people sometimes seek out the church later in life when they are ready to get married or when they have children of their own for whom they feel a responsibility to provide a Christian upbringing. One of the purposes of the rite of Affirmation of Baptism in the *Lutheran Book of Worship* (Pew edition, page 198ff.) is "Restoration to Membership," and similar purposes are seen for the reaffirmation of the baptismal covenant within the Liturgy of Holy Baptism in *The Book of Common Prayer* of the Episcopal Church (page 303). The new United Methodist and Presbyterian Hymnals provide a rite such as "Affirmation of Baptism" for those who are being received into membership in the congregation from other denominations, as does the *Lutheran Book of Worship.* We should recognize that even those joining a congregation from another denominational background have probably experienced a time of lapse or rupture in their participation in their previous church life. Ritualization of

140

the process of return to the community of faith, or changing one's identification with a particular fellowship in the gospel, and its accompanying catechesis, has not been as amply developed as that for Christian initiation. But the R.C.I.A. provides a model and also materials for working with the restoration of the lapsed. For example, *Invitation: A Catholic Learning Guide for Adults*, prepared by Alfred McBride, O. Praem,[9] is intended to be used in:

- The Rite of Christian Initiation of Adults
- Adult Inquiry Forums for Non-Catholics
- Reconciling Inactive Catholics
- Parish Adult Formation Programs

We will address in greater detail the content of such an adult catechumenate in the following chapter.

In the meantime we also continue to baptize the children of Christian families. In many cases this is a very natural thing to do because of the level of participation in the life of the church already practiced by the family which presents its child for baptism. But since baptism does presuppose a relationship with the community of faith (underscored by calling it "Christian initiation"), we can no longer be as indiscriminate in our practice of infant baptism as the church once was. There should be some assurance that the baptized child will have a continuing relationship with the community of faith so that faith may be nurtured. This will require pastoral counseling with Christian parents before the time of the baptism and continuing formation in the faith for the child after baptism as provided in the educational and pastoral ministry of the congregation. Those who are most likely able to carry out the promise that the child will be brought to the services of God's house, taught the basics of the catechism, given the scriptures, and provided with instruction in the Christian faith, are the ones who should serve as the baptismal sponsors, and in most cases these people will be the child's parents, not favorite aunts and uncles or the parents' best friends from an earlier stage in their lives.

A parish thus has three simultaneous evangelism programs to attend to: the preparation of adults for baptism, the preparation of previously-baptized adults for affirmation of their baptism, and the preparation of parents for the baptism of their infants or young children. A joint Episcopal-Lutheran training program in "The Catechumenal Process" has been developed by the Office of Evangelism Ministries of The Episcopal Church.[10] The following chart indicates how "The Catechumenal Process" addresses the needs of a diverse group of people who seek a more mature Christian commitment and discipleship.

It is evident that this program is based on the R.C.I.A. It draws upon an important element of Episcopal and Lutheran liturgical spirituality in that it is related to the church year, specifically to Lent, holy week, and Easter. The rite of "Enrollment of Candidates for Baptism" is held on the First Sunday in Lent. Such a rite is the very first order in *Occasional Services: A Companion to Lutheran Book of Worship.*[11] There is no reason why this rite of enrollment could not be used with infant as well as adult candidates for baptism and that all baptisms from this time on be "stored up" for the Easter vigil. Ash Wednesday is the occasion for "The Calling of the Baptized to Continuing Conversion," but it is specifically aimed at those who need to be restored to the life and mission of the church after a time of lapsed membership. In earlier times these "returnees" would have been penitents seeking sacramental reconciliation. They would have been dressed in sackcloth and ashes and dismissed along with the catechumens before the liturgy of the faithful. This is not how we would want to treat our "returnees" today; moreover, we may have a real need to retrieve the ancient order of penitents for reasons suited to its original purposes. But this does

THE CATECHUMENAL PROCESS
FOUR STAGES

Preparation of Adults for Holy Baptism: The Catechumenate	Preparation of Baptized Persons for Reaffirmation of the Baptismal Covenant	Preparation of Parents for the Baptism of Infants and Young Children
STAGE ONE		
Stage Pre-Catechumenal Period	**Stage** Inquiry	**Stage** Pregnancy
Rite Admission of Catechumens	**Rite** The Welcoming of Baptized Christians into a Community	**Rite** The Blessing of Parents at the Beginning of Pregnancy
STAGE TWO		
Stage The Catechumenate	**Stage** Formation period--deeper exploration of faith and ministry	**Stage** Pregnancy to Birth/Preparation for Adoption
Rite First Sunday in Lent: Enrollment of Candidates for Baptism	**Rite** Ash Wednesday: The Calling of the Baptized to Continuing Conversion	**Rite** Thanksgiving for the Birth or Adoption of a Child
STAGE THREE		
Stage Candidacy for Baptism	**Stage** Preparation for Reaffirmation of the Baptismal Covenant at Easter	**Stage** Preparation for Baptism
Rite Lent III,IV,V: Prayers for the Candidates; Presentation of Creeds and Lord's Prayer	**Rite** Maundy Thursday Rite of Preparation for the Paschal Holy Days	**Rite**
HOLY BAPTISM at the Easter Vigil	*REAFFIRMATION OF THE BAPTISMAL COVENANT* at the Easter Vigil; Presentation to the Bishop for Laying on of Hands: Confirmation and Reception	*HOLY BAPTISM*
STAGE FOUR		
Stage Great Fifty Days of Easter: Mystagogy; Post-Baptismal Catechesis	**Stage** Great Fifty Days of Easter: Joining with those baptized at the Vigil in Post-Baptismal Catechesis	**Stage** Continuing formation and exploration of the mysteries of the faith

Prepared By The Rev. Walter L. Guettsche & The Rev. Ann E .P. McElligott

provide a model for working with the lapsed since it aims at re-formation in the faith.

As with R.C.I.A., the season of Lent is the time for intense work with those preparing for baptism as well as those who are to be restored or received into church membership. On the Sundays of Lent III, IV, and V the Creeds and the Lord's Prayer are "presented" to the catechumens and they are prayed for in the intercessions. While the "returnees" or "prospective members" are included along with the catechumens in faith formation and acts of ministry, their prior initiation needs to be respected. In the meantime the pastor is meeting with parents and sponsors of infants and young children who are to be baptized. This all comes to culmination at the Easter vigil.

But as with R.C.I.A., this does not end the process. During the Great Fifty Days of Easter the post-baptismal catechesis takes place. Those who have affirmed their baptism at the Easter vigil join in this mystagogical instruction with the newly baptized, and there may be continuing formation and exploration of the faith with the parents of infant neophytes. At some point in this season, when the mystagogy is finished, the newly baptized remove their white robes and join the rest of the faithful. We recall that for Augustine this was an occasion for exhortation to the newly baptized that they should be, in effect, the leaven which raises the whole lump of Christians.

It should be considered that if we are describing a process in which those going through catechesis are enrolled at the beginning of Lent, a certain amount of evangelistic activity would have to happen before Ash Wednesday. As with the R.C.I.A., we can envision a "precatechumenate" extending back into the weeks after the Epiphany. This is the time when the congregation's evangelists would be busy extending invitations to baptism or renewed membership to those who have become regular at worship and other activities in the congregation. We assume that these are people who have long since been welcomed into the life of the church and exposed to its purposes and teachings. We cannot help but notice the parallel between recruiting candidates for the catechumenate during the weeks after the Epiphany and some of the Sunday gospels of this season which tell of Jesus' recruitment of disciples at the beginning of his ministry. Indeed, the catechumenal process envisions the enrollment of candidates during the precatechumenal stage, although perhaps the actual public rite of enrollment is held off until the beginning of Lent.

Is this the only time in the church year that such a process should be going on? We recall that in the ancient Roman church, Pentecost was a second great day for public baptism. Pentecost was usually the day on which to celebrate the baptisms of those who, for whatever reasons, were not able to be baptized at the Easter vigil, and for that reason Pentecost has its own vigil. In the more recent past Pentecost has also become a time for confirmation, which is now redefined as the first solemn affirmation of baptism by those who were baptized as infants or young children. This part of the long-term continuing formation and exploration of the faith should not be neglected. Tradition, at least in the Reformation churches, supports the intensive pastoral and educational work, often of two or three years' duration, with the adolescent members of the parish. We need to be modest in our assessment of what can be accomplished with young people who are betwixt-and-between childhood and adulthood, and who may be in this liminoid existence for years to come in our society. They are not in a state in which they can make mature and lasting commitments. But experiences and encounters during this formative time in their lives can leave lasting impressions. There cannot be a separation between cognition, or rational knowledge, and the affections, or emotions, in our presentation of the faith—with adolescents or with anyone else! Relationships with leaders and peers and ritual expres-

145

sions of passage make as much impact on the confirmands as the information transmitted in the classroom. Liturgy and experiences of hospitality and inclusion play a role every bit as crucial as teaching and instruction in our work with confirmands and with all other catechumens. If there are some "left-over" candidates for baptism at Pentecost, it would provide a fitting opportunity for the confirmands to affirm their baptism in the context of a baptismal celebration and even prepare for the celebration along with the baptismal candidates in preparation for their role, as mature Christians, as sponsors of baptism.

In the eastern and Hispanic churches, Epiphany was the second great day for public baptism. Certainly the Sunday after the Epiphany, the Baptism of our Lord, lends itself to such an occasion. Historically, however, there was a problem in maintaining a process of initiation similar to that during Lent, once the Christmas season intervened between Advent and Epiphany. Christmas does not lend itself to ritualizing conversion the same way that holy week does; it is a time of feasting, not of fasting. It appears that the original Advent season in the Gallican and Hispanic liturgical books was a six-week season beginning near St. Martin's Day, November 11, and hence called "St. Martin's Lent." It had baptismal and penitential overtones. But our present Advent season projects an eschatological thrust and leads into the celebration of the incarnation. However, fall is often a time when new families come into the congregation and young children who are presented for baptism in the late fall might be "stored up" for a baptismal festival on the Sunday after the Epiphany when, in connection with the baptism of Jesus, the baptismal theme of adoption might be highlighted.

Thus, we are envisioning an initiation season that is as follows: Epiphany—recruitment of candidates for baptism or affirmation of baptism; Lent—enrollment of candidates, catechesis and praxis; Easter vigil—baptism and affirmation of baptism; Easter—mystagogical catechesis; Day of Pentecost—baptism and affirmation of baptism (confirmation).

What becomes of the rest of the year? The time after Pentecost is the time of mission in which we evangelize in "the joy and peace of the Holy Spirit." The time over the summer months and into the fall is devoted to advertising the faith and the community of faith and inviting people to "come and see," without the pressure of having to decide whether or not to join the church. During the fall inquiry classes would be set up in which the church's basic teachings and the faith stories of its members can be shared. This is not a time when commitment is asked for. It is a time to present the gospel and lead inquirers into its fellowship. The approach of the Christmas season gives inquirers an opportunity to experience the liturgical life of the church at its full festivity, with all of the power of ritual and symbol to make an impact and project a vision of what life in this world can be in anticipation of the life of the world to come. Then, after the Epiphany, the invitation to membership is issued to those who need to be baptized or to affirm their baptism.

Why this emphasis on the *time* of Christian initiation? To ask what significance certain times have for doing certain things is like asking whether symbols are "merely symbolic." If symbols somehow participate in the reality to which they point, our celebrations of certain days and seasons link us with that which these days and seasons proclaim. And that helps us to keep in perspective our evangelistic task. Our task is not just to gain new members for the church; it is to proclaim what God has done in the life, death, resurrection, and ascension of Jesus the Christ, his only Son, our Lord, as that is unfolded in the church-year calendar and lectionary. It may be that membership growth and gospel proclamation are not mutually exclusive, but that is finally up to the Holy Spirit who works faith when and where he chooses. Our task is simply to be faithful to our commission: "Go . . . and make disciples of all nations . . . baptizing them . . . and teaching them to obey everything that I have commanded you. And remember, I am with you always, to the end of the age" (Mt 28:18–20, New RSV).

Christian Initiation: A Task for the Territorial Church

The strategic task of making Christians has employed different tactics over the course of the centuries. Initially, the task was to integrate Gentile converts into Jewish messianic communities. But with the influx of Gentile converts Christianity became more of a counter-cultural and illicit cult within the Greco-Roman world (the age of Hippolytus and Tertullian). The situation of intermittent persecution affected the church's initiation policies and required the institution of sponsorship and the practice of scrutinizing the candidates. By the fourth and fifth centuries Christianity had emerged as a licit and then as an established religion in the Roman Empire. This new situation required the church to develop highly articulated ritual processes by which to preserve some of the fervor of earlier practices in a situation in which the demands for baptism left the church pastorally breathless. In the wake of the collapse of the Roman Empire, Christian missionary activity was directed toward conveying both the gospel and classical civilization to the barbarian Teutonic, Nordic and Slavic peoples. This created the culture of Christendom in which the task of Christian formation was accomplished by a partnership of church and society. This partnership has been dissolving since the time of the Renaissance, and has just about come to the point of termination as we approach the end of the twentieth century. Nevertheless, we must recognize that the different missionary situations in which the church finds itself in different places around the world call for different tactics.

The retrieval of the ancient Christian practices of initiation captured in the Roman Catholic Church's Rite of Christian Initiation of Adults (1972) can be most thoroughly implemented in places where adult conversions are not only the "norm" in the sense of "standard," as clarified by Aidan Kavanagh,[1] but also the "norm" in the sense of "frequency" of practice and numbers. This is certainly the case where no previous experience of Christendom exists, such as in the countries of Africa and Asia. In countries where Christendom has existed, such as in Europe, and even more so in countries where the culture of Christendom has been imported, such as in North and South America and Australia, the R.C.I.A. can achieve only limited success. Not surprisingly, the successes have been mostly in urban parishes where generations of unbaptized adults can be found in surrounding communities. With the collapse of the militantly anti-religious regimes in eastern Europe and in the former Soviet Union, a situation now exists which can only be compared to the time of the church's "coming out" into society during the era of Constantine. Not since that time has the church faced the task of absorbing such large numbers of adult converts whose motives for coming into the church may be as much political and fashion as faith. If the leaders of these churches, faced with hundreds and even thousands of requests for baptism each year, do not implement in some way a viable catechumenate, an opportunity will be missed for providing an enduring Christian vitality beyond the immediate euphoria of the collapse of the Communist empire.

The churches in North America face a different kind of situation. We live in societies which are officially secular (in terms of the separation of church and state), but which have experienced historically a Christian cultural hegemony that is now dissolving as a result of the increasing religious pluralism in our society. While the culture of Christendom could not be officially maintained in our society, it has been preserved for generations in the subcultural enclaves that make up our local parishes. In these situations the medieval initiation policy can be maintained, as can be seen in the fact that child candidates for baptism vastly outnumber adult candidates. But even these parishes cannot ignore the need to deal with converts, either in the case of unbaptized youth and adults or in the case of baptized youth and adults in need of serious faith formation.

Kavanagh has stated that the medieval initiation policy was directed "not so much at conversion of those outside the faith as at conversion of those within the Church to lives of greater piety and more intense devotion. . . ."[2] In this model conversion was not associated with baptism, since the candidates for baptism were usually infants; it was associated more with novitiates in the religious orders and with seminary education. Even for Protestants, the seminaries became surrogate catechumenates where those with white-hot conversion experiences were sent to have their experiences cooled down by theological study and pastoral practice in order that their lives of faith would be of more practical benefit to the church. The only thing that has changed in recent years is that students who have less experience of the empirical life of the church than was previously the case are enrolling in seminaries; they have more wrenching changes in their lives, since they tend to be older and already established in a career. On the other hand, the falling off of seminary matriculations indicates that seminary is seen less and less as a viable option for those who return to the life of the church after a time of absence. This suggests that, whether we are dealing with adult candidates for baptism or the return of adults who have been away from the church since adolescence, the kind of faith formation provided by seminaries for their students (reluctantly, in many cases) now needs to be provided for adult members of our congregations.

What follows is a schema of how this faith formation can be done in the context of Christian initiation. Whether we are dealing with those who need to be baptized or those who need to affirm their baptism, we need to attend to the processes of doctrinal formation, life in the Christian community, engagement in the work of the community, and participation in the community's worship. There has been considerable reflection on the experience of Christian initiation in the Roman Catholic Church.[3] To that I add my own pastoral reflections.

An important observation is that the parish may not be the setting in which the Christian initiation or faith formation of adults is best accomplished. In Roman Catholic parishes pastors have become overburdened because of the shortage of priests. They could not be expected to give the kind of attention and energy to the R.C.I.A. that it requires. In Protestant congregations, which are usually much smaller in membership (counting hundreds of members rather than thousands of families), there are usually not a sufficient number of adult candidates for baptism or for faith formation which would justify the time and energy that must be devoted to the catechumenal process. The reader should understand that by making this statement I am not saying that the necessary time and energy should not be given to this task. I am simply making a realistic assessment of what is likely to be the case. The fact that Protestant pastors have fewer individual members to care for than Roman Catholic priests does not mean that their workload is lighter than that of the priests. A smaller ratio of pastors to members means that the expectations of pastoral care are higher in Protestant than in Roman Catholic parishes. One also notes that although R.C.I.A. has been in existence for twenty years now, it has still not been implemented in the majority of Roman Catholic parishes. One doubts that this is due merely to sloth. It is more likely the case that the structure of the R.C.I.A. is so ecologically whole that it cannot be introduced piecemeal; and to attempt to introduce it at all is a staggering task which also challenges the parochial status quo. This observation should give pause to any attempt to introduce it in non-Roman Catholic churches, except that there is simply no other strategy available for "making Christians" that is as evangelistically and liturgically sound as the R.C.I.A. and any initiatory process based upon it.

The answer to this dilemma, it seems to me, lies in the polity of the ancient church in which this model of Christian initiation arose. It simply was not the case in the churches of the Roman Empire that Christian initiation was a parochial concern.[4] The bishop was the chief minister of initiation and supervised the catechumenal process in the metropolitan church. The retention of the episcopal prerogative to perform the rite of confirmation in the western church is at least partially a survival of the tradition of episcopal responsibility for Christian initiation. The bishop came around to parishes to "confirm" the baptisms performed there in his absence. This suggests that the locus of the supervision of Christian initiation should not be the parish but the diocese/synod/district/conference (whatever the appropriate local judicatory might be called). The proposal we shall develop here will take this into account, which means that it also assails congregational autonomy.

On the other hand, the R.C.I.A. and the catechumenal process must involve the worshiping community. For one thing, sponsors and godparents of catechumens should be those who can "shepherd" the catechumen into the life and mission of the church. Secondly, the life and mission of the church must be tangibly experienced, which means that it will be primarily experienced on the parochial level. So this proposal will build a relationship between the church parochial and the church territorial in a joint program of Christian initiation and adult faith formation.

The component parts of the catechumenal process must include:

—a catechumenal school in which doctrinal instruction takes place under the tutelage of competent catechists;
—integration into the life and mission of the congregation under the supervision of sponsors or godparents;
—opportunities to engage in works of ministry either in the local congregation or in agencies and institutions of the judicatory; and
—regular participation in the worship of the local congregation as well as in the rites marking moments of transition in the catechumenate which might be presided over by the bishop or some episcopally-delegated minister.

It is perhaps necessary to point out that one of the side effects of the implementation of the R.C.I.A. or the catechumenal process is to reintegrate what have become distinct ministries in the church: evangelism, education, social ministry and worship. Nor is it a matter of saying that one or another of these has priority of place in the scheme of Christian initiation. While evangelism is not education, and education is not social ministry, and social ministry is not worship, and worship is none of the above—all of these activities together are necessary to accomplish the task of faith formation. This means that we cannot have evangelists who are unconcerned about education, social ministry, or worship; or Christian educators who are unconcerned about liturgy or social ministry. If a certain primacy accrues to liturgy, it is only because of the sacramental character of Christian initiation. But all western Christians need to see sacramental reality as larger than we usually do so that, with Augustine, we can see even such sacramental rites as the signing with the cross and the giving of salt as sacramenta prefiguring baptism and the eucharist.[5]

With this in mind, let us attend first to the catechumenal school.

This school might be provided by the judicatory as a center to which all the parishes can send their candidates. A central location would obviously work well in a metropolitan judicatory. Judicatories which embrace larger geographic areas might need several centers. The teachers or catechists would be salaried professionals who devote full time to this ministry. Not just any competent theologian would do as a teacher. The catechumenate involves not just the transmission of doctrine but conversion therapy. The catechist is not just conveying information but leading the candidates through a change that involves renunciation of the worldview and values of "this world" and adherence to Christ and the life of the world to come. The content of the catechumenal school is also special. It is not just biblical, theological and ethical study (although all that is included); it is the content of the catechism.

The catechism is the church's handbook for the instruction of catechumens. It contains the most basic things a Christian needs to know and to be able to draw upon in a deliberate Christian life. Lutherans especially are familiar with the Catechism and catechetical instruction because of

155

familiarity with Martin Luther's Catechisms (Small and Large).[6] But these were patterned after medieval catechisms and a tradition that extends all the way back to antiquity. The handing over of the four gospels, the Creed, and the Lord's Prayer in the mass of the scrutinies in the Gelasian Sacramentary constitutes a catechism.[7]

What Luther included in his Catechisms was and is still the essential content of the catechumenate in its various stages: the ten commandments, the Creed, the Lord's Prayer, baptism, penance, and eucharist. The ten commandments relate to the precatechumenate when persons are "seeking" after God's will for them and the world. The Creed and Lord's Prayer are presented during the Period of Enlightenment when one is being entrusted with the content of the faith in preparation for baptism. The discussion of baptism and the eucharist occur during the period of mystagogy following the reception of the sacraments of initiation. Luther understood penance, or the office of the keys, as a "return to baptism" and therefore as a way of living out the baptismal life.

The catechism cannot be and probably never has been taught without reference to important questions also raised by the catechumen or the world out of which she or he comes. The catechumenal school will present the catechism in a "large" way rather than a "small" way (such as Lutherans regularly do in the confirmation ministry with young adolescents, in which the Small Catechism has remained the basic textbook around which other curricula are developed). The basic texts, of course, are to be installed in the mind through memorization whether the catechism is "large" or "small". But a "large catechism" will also venture into more speculative areas.[8]

Fleshed out here is one possible course using the basic texts of the catechism so that it is possible to demonstrate the extent of catechumenal instruction. The school might begin in the fall with the ten commandments and sessions as follows:

1. The concept of torah: the life-giving word of God in creation, in the law of Moses, in the fulfillment of the law in Christ.
2. "I am the Lord your God who brought you out of Egypt." The doctrine of election: the election of Israel and baptismal election.
3. The first commandment: What does it mean to have a god? What candidates for "god" are there?
4. The second commandment: How shall we call upon the true God?
5. The third commandment: How shall we show devotion to the God who creates, redeems and sanctifies us?
6. The fourth commandment: What authorities has God established for the governance of the world, and how shall they be honored?
7. The fifth commandment: How shall we respect God-given life in the various ethical dilemmas we face in this world (e.g., wars, police action, abortion, euthanasia, etc.)?
8. The sixth commandment: How shall we respect the covenant of marriage (ours and other people's)?
9. The seventh commandment: How shall we respect our neighbor's property? Of what value is honesty and integrity in this world?
10. The eighth commandment: How shall we respect and preserve the reputations of others? What is truth?
11. The ninth commandment: How shall we respect our neighbor's spouse and possessions? How can we be content with the blessings we have received from God?
12. The tenth commandment: How shall we respect our

neighbor's employees? Here the doctrine of vocation might be developed.

At this point we are approaching the Advent-Christmas season, and the catechumens should be introduced to the four canonical gospels. How does each gospel preserve a unique witness to the life, message, and saving action of Jesus Christ?

After Christmas, it is time to consider the Creed in four sessions:

1. The role of creeds: The doctrine of the Trinity.
2. The article on creation: God as creator; the world as creation.
3. The article on redemption: God as redeemer in Jesus Christ; the doctrine of atonement.
4. The article on sanctification: God as Spirit who brings about new life; church, forgiveness, resurrection of the body, eternal life.

Following the study of the Creed as the expression of the church's faith, the catechumenal curriculum moves on to the prayer in which faith is expressed. The following sessions might be offered:

1. What is prayer? Why the Lord's Prayer? What is its biblical background and historical use?
2. The name of God. How shall God be addressed in prayer?
3. The kingdom of God. Where does God rule?
4. The will of God. How do we know what it is? How can it be done? The doctrine of predestination might come up here and should be squarely faced as the way the sovereignty of God's will has been affirmed.
5. "Daily Bread" or "Tomorrow's Bread Today"? Bread for the world and a foretaste of the feast to come.

6. Forgiveness in a community of reconciliation.
7. Times of trial: faith put to the test.
8. The reality, persistence, and defeat of evil.
9. The praise of God in liturgy and life (doxology).

At this point we are most likely into Lent and the time during which the four gospels, the Creed, and the Lord's Prayer will be delivered to the catechumens in the Sunday liturgies in their congregations. Special homilies on the Sundays or weekdays in Lent might be devoted to the following topics:

- Lent I—A Testing of Faith (with reference to the testing of Christ in the wilderness)
- Lent II—The Four Gospels: Testimonies of Faith
- Lent III—The Creed: The Identity of Faith
- Lent IV—The Lord's Prayer: The Cry of Faith
- Lent V—The "Return" (Recitation) of These Texts: The Act of Faith. The candidates recite the Creed and Lord's Prayer in the presence of the congregation.

The catechumens are receiving this instruction and are prayed for in their parish churches during Lent. The initiatory character of this process would be underscored if the catechumens were dismissed after the liturgy of the word with a blessing. This would indicate that inclusion in the eucharistic fellowship is the goal of Christian initiation. We will propose that baptism take place at a vigil at the cathedral or in some other place where the whole territorial church may assemble. But after receiving the sacraments of initiation (baptism, confirmation, first communion), the neophytes return to the catechumenal school for the mystagogical catechsis (which would be reinforced liturgically by the homilies and eucharistic celebrations in their congregations). It is at this point that the catechists

159

deal with baptism, penance, and the Lord's supper. As time permits in the seven weeks until Pentecost, other "marks of the church" might be covered in the catechumenal school, such as the doctrine of the word of God, the doctrine of the church, the historic liturgy, and ordained/lay ministries. A summer session of the catechumenal school might be devoted to Bible study and practice in witnessing to one's faith in daily life and work.

The second area that requires thought is the context of Christian initiation in the Easter vigil.[9] The problem is that, for all the high-sounding words we use to promote the Easter vigil, it has not taken off. I have been involved as a pastoral leader of the vigil for over twenty years in five different congregations, and the vigil has not yet made it in parochial consciousness, except among a few die-hard devotees. All sorts of arrangements have been made to try to make it more popular. Some Protestant congregations have tried to celebrate it as their sunrise service—beginning before dawn. Unfortunately, nature doesn't cooperate. It becomes light too soon, and the whole light-of-Christ-shining-in-the-darkness motif of the vigil is lost. This becomes a reminder that it was possible for the early church, and our Eastern Orthodox brothers and sisters, to begin the vigil at midnight (originally in Asia Minor this was when the Jewish Passover ended) and conclude with baptism and eucharist at dawn.

The other option is to begin the vigil at an earlier hour on Saturday night. But parishes are so preoccupied with handling the Easter crowds on Sunday, with special music and breakfasts, that the tendency is to rush through it, usually reducing the number of readings, and thus losing the vigil character of the service. A suggestion has been made to hold the light service and the vigil readings on Saturday night, ending with a litany, and then reconvening early Easter morning for the renewal of baptism and the first eucharist of Easter. But the few hours of sleep will seem like an unwanted intrusion on a great spiritual experience, and some of the worshipers might be lost to other activities and responsibilities between Saturday night and Sunday morning.

The Easter vigil will probably remain obscure until at least all adult baptisms are celebrated at that time only. In my experience, the vigils with highest attendance were those with baptisms and confirmations. Some parishes, however, can't come up with an adult candidate for baptism in the course of a year, and I will confess my own timidity at suggesting to parents that they have their children baptized in the middle of the night, or even late Saturday evening (although I think that would come if we first had adult baptisms at the vigil).

The proposal of a diocesan or synodical catechumenal school suggests another approach to the vigil. This requires ending the parochial observance of the vigil and joining together with other congregations for a joint observance. There are any number of ways to do this. Churches with bishops might consider planning a diocesan or synodical celebration of the vigil in a large place of assembly (either a very big church or a sports arena). This was done by the Roman Catholic diocese of Duluth in 1971, which filled the Duluth Arena with 7500 worshipers (out of a Roman Catholic population of 20,000). I don't know what the subsequent impact was of that experience, but it makes sense for those who have attended the catechetical school together to be baptized together at the bishop's vigil. I am also aware of some ecumenical joint celebrations, for example between Lutherans and Episcopalians and among Presbyterians, Methodists, and the United Church of Christ. No matter what the form of the joint celebration, a further necessity is that parishes do not schedule early morning Easter day services. Those who attend the vigil are worshiping on Easter day because the liturgical day begins on its Eve at Vespers. Finally, there would be enough time to

161

schedule at least two fullsome Easter morning services for those who did not attend the vigil. Those baptized at this joint vigil should be present at an Easter day service and at the service on the following Sunday, wearing their white robes (albs), to be congratulated by the rest of the congregation. Thanksgiving for their sacramental incorporation into the body of Christ should be included in the parish intercessions on Easter day and Easter II.

No matter what format the vigil takes, preparation is absolutely crucial. This can be done in parishes by emphasizing the renewal of baptism during Lent. One way is to make use of the vigil readings as texts for Bible study and mid-week sermons during Lent and to use the accompanying collects as a way of drawing out the baptismal implications of each text.[10] Children can also be involved in considering the meaning of their baptisms by studying it in church school classes. Some very evocative texts are included in the vigil readings which will appeal to children and adults alike. Parish artists might be recruited to design banners utilizing these biblical texts and baptismal themes. The point is that "the greatest feast" will not be the greatest feast until there is a massive effort through catechesis to prepare people to celebrate it well. Our half-hearted efforts up until now have not worked, and the whole church has been the poorer for it because it has missed out on the celebration of the cosmos-shaking event of Jesus' passover from death to life. This is the gospel event to which the church makes witness, and that witness is less than it might be without recourse to its liturgical celebration in the "queen of feasts."

This proposal of a joint effort at catechesis and a joint celebration of initiation does not relieve the local church of its responsibilities in these areas. The invitation into the fellowship of the gospel, the recruitment of candidates for the catechumenate, the shepherding of new members into the life of the church is the responsibility of the parish church. Sponsors should be appointed from the congregation with which these new members will affiliate, and these sponsors should accompany their candidates to all rites celebrated by the catechumenal school as well as in the congregation. Certainly a large delegation from the candidate's congregation should accompany him or her to the joint celebration of the Easter vigil. During the catechumenate, those preparing for baptism should be included by name in the intercessions of the congregation. On Easter day and on the Second Sunday of Easter those baptized at the bishop's vigil should be included in the thanksgivings of the congregation. There might also be a parish party to celebrate their baptism. In these ways the relationship between the new members and their congregation will thoroughly established.

The possibilities of joint catechesis and celebration raises the possibility of joint efforts in evangelism. One would think that it would be possible for pastors of neighboring parishes, at least within a denomination, to share prospective member lists so that maximum care is given to those who are seeking to join a community of faith. The next step would be for pastors of different denominations to share their prospective member lists. The kind of denominational cooperation which missionaries in Africa have experienced should also be the case in North America. The entrepreneurial spirit which results in competition for members and results in the fracturing of the body of Christ needs to be curtailed in the interests of the mission of the gospel. After all, the churches already recognize baptism administered in churches other than their own. If the act of initiation can be commonly recognized and jointly celebrated, the processes leading to it can also be joint efforts and the celebrations issuing from it can be common expressions of fellowship. The eucharist, as the central expression of Christian fellowship and mission, not only seals the unity that already exists but effects unity. It is a means of grace. When it is celebrated ecumenically the eucharist will most forcefully effect that reconciliation that is at the heart of God's mission to the world, and the worshiping community will best bear witness to the divine intention.

Notes

WORSHIP AND WITNESS: TENSIONS AND RELATIONSHIPS

1. J. G. Davies, *Worship and Mission* (London: SCM Press, 1966).

2. Peter Brunner, *Worship in the Name of Jesus,* trans. Martin H. Bertram (St. Louis: Concordia Publishing House, 1968), pp. 11ff.

3. Octavius, 32; in *The Fathers of the Church* (New York, 1950), X, 389.

4. Alexander Schmemann, *Introduction to Liturgical Theology* (London: The Faith Press, 1966), p. 73.

5. Ignatius, *Epistle to the Romans* 4:1–2; in *Early Christian Fathers: The Library of Christian Classics,* I, trans. and ed. Cyril C. Richardson (Philadelphia: The Westminster Press, 1953), p. 104.

6. *Romans* 7:3; *Early Christian Fathers,* p. 104.

7. *Martyrdom of Polycarp* 14–15; *Early Christian Fathers,* pp. 154–55.

8. Cited in Louis Bouyer, *The Spirituality of the New Testament and the Fathers: History of Christian Spirituality,* I, English trans. (New York, Tournai, Paris, Rome: Desclée Company, 1963), p. 207.

9. Ibid., p. 208.

10. Alexander Schmemann, *For the Life of the World* (St. Vladimir's Seminary Press, 1974), p. 103.

11. See the chapter on "Frontier Worship" in James F. White, *Protestant Worship: Traditions in Transition* (Louisville: Westminster/John Knox Press, 1989) for the development of a liturgical style which has had a profound affect on Protestant worship in North America.

12. Quoted from the brochure advertising the seminar.

13. See M. Douglas Meeks, "Speaking the Gospel Publicly in North America," in *Liturgy: A Life to Share* (Washington, D.C.: The Liturgical Conference, 1991), pp. 9–15.

14. Robert Bellah et al., *Habits of the Heart* (University of California, 1984).

15. Quentin J. Schultze, *Televangelism and American Culture—The Business of Popular Religion* (Grand Rapids: Baker Book House, 1991), p. 95.

16. Neil Postman, *Amusing Ourselves to Death* (New York: Viking Press, 1985), p. 121.

17. Walter P. Kallestad, "Entertainment Evangelism," *The Lutheran* 3 (May 23, 1990), pp. 17ff.

18. Schultze, p. 211.

THE CHARACTER OF WORSHIP: CORRUPTIONS OF PRACTICE

1. Paul Waitman Hoon, *The Integrity of Worship* (Nashville: Abingdon Press, 1973), pp. 52ff.

2. Lawrence A. Hoffman, *The Art of Public Prayer: Not for Clergy Only* (Washington, D.C.: The Liturgical Press, 1988), pp. 81–82.

3. Joseph Sittler, *The Care of the Earth and Other University Sermons* (Philadelphia: Fortress Press, 1964), pp. 121ff.

4. Hoon, pp. 63ff.

5. Ernst Cassirer, *An Essay on Man: An Introduction to a Philosophy of Human Culture* (New Haven: Yale University Press, 1944), p. 26.

6. Cited in Gerhard Kappner, "The Church Service

and Music," *The Scottish Journal of Theology* 12 (1959), 248–49.

7. Jaroslav Pelikan, *Fools for Christ* (Philadelphia: Muhlenberg Press, 1955), p. 152.

8. Gerhard van der Leeuw, *Sacred and Profane Beauty: The Holy in Art*, trans. David E. Green (Nashville: Abingdon Press, 1963), pp. 163–64.

9. David Power, "Liturgy, Memory and the Absence of God," *Worship* 57 (1983), 328.

10. Geoffrey Wainwright, *Doxology: The Praise of God in Worship, Doctrine and Life* (New York: Oxford University Press, 1980), p. 42.

11. Dietrich Bonhoeffer, *Letters and Papers from Prison*, rev. ed. (London: SCM Press, 1967), letter of July 16, 1944.

12. "An Order of Mass and Communion for the Church at Wittenberg," *Luther's Works*, American Ed. (Philadelphia: Fortress Press, 1965), Vol. 53, p. 19.

THE MISSION OF THE CHURCH: DEFECTIVE
CONCEPTS OF EVANGELISM

1. Roland Allen, *The Ministry of the Spirit*, ed. David M. Paton (Grand Rapids: Wm. B. Eerdmans, 1960), p. 17.

2. Dietrich Bonhoeffer, *Ethics*, ed. Eberhard Bethge (New York: Macmillan, 1955), p. 297.

3. D. T. Niles, *Upon the Earth: The Mission of God and the Missionary Enterprize of the Church* (New York: McGraw-Hill, 1962), p. 52.

4. Alexander Schmemann, *For the Life of the World* (St. Vladimir's Seminary Press, 1974), p. 14.

5. Walter Freytag, "The Meaning and Purpose of the Christian Mission," *International Review of Missions* 39 (1950), 159.

6. Gibson Winter, *The New Creation as Metropolis* (New York: Macmillan, 1963), p. 19.

7. Gibson Winter, *The Suburban Captivity of the Church* (Garden City, N.J.: Doubleday, 1961), p. 163.

8. Winter, *The New Creation*, p. 15.

9. *Ibid.*, p. 16.

10. A. R. Vidler, *God's Demand and Man's Response* (1938), pp. 77f., quoted in John Baillie, *Baptism and Conversion* (New York: Scribner, 1963), p. 110.

11. Paul Tillich, *Systematic Theology*, I (Chicago: University of Chicago Press, 1951), 49.

12. J. V. Taylor, *The Primal Vision: Christian Presence Amid African Religion* (Philadelphia: Fortress, 1963), p. 172.

13. *Ibid.*, p. 178.

14. See J. Lofland and R. Stark, "Becoming a World-Saver: A Theory of Conversion to a Deviant Perspective," *American Sociological Review* 30 (1965), 862–874; also J. Lofland, *Doomsday Cult* (Englewood Cliffs, NJ: Prentice-Hall, 1966). See also the appendix, "Paul's Conversion: Psychological Study," in Alan F. Segal, *Paul the Convert: The Apostolate and Apostasy of Saul the Pharisee* (New Haven and London: Yale University Press, 1990), pp. 285–300. Segal distinguishes between "call" and "conversion" and holds that conversion entails a change in one's religious community, for which a choice must be available.

15. Aidan Kavanagh, "Christian Initiation: Tactics and Strategy," in *Made, Not Born: New Perspectives on Christian Initiation and the Catechumenate*, Murphy Center for Liturgical Research (Notre Dame, IN: University of Notre Dame Press, 1976), p. 3.

16. See *The Treatise on The Apostolic Tradition of St. Hippolytus of Rome*, ed. and trans. Gregory Dix (London: S.P.C.K., 1937; reprinted 1968), p. 30.

17. Frederic van der Meer, *Augustine the Bishop*, trans.

B. Battershaw and G. R. Lamb (London: Sheed and Ward, 1961), p. 381.

18. Freytag, *art. cit.*, pp. 159ff.

19. James A. Scherer, *Missionary, Go Home!* (Englewood Cliffs, NJ: Prentice-Hall, 1964), p. 133.

20. J. C. Hoekendijk, "On Proselytism," *Monthly Letter About Evangelism* 3/4 (March/April 1961), 8.

THE WITNESS OF BAPTISM: PASSAGE AND TRANSFORMATION

1. Alexander Schmemann, *For the Life of the World* (St. Vladimir's Seminary Press, 1974), p. 67.

2. Aidan Kavanagh, "Christian Initiation of Adults: The Rites," in *Made, Not Born: New Perspectives on Christian Initiation and the Catechumenate.* Murphy Center for Liturgical Research (Notre Dame: University of Notre Dame Press, 1976), p. 125.

3. Rudolf Schnackenburg, *Baptism in the Thought of St. Paul*, trans. G. R. Beasley-Murray (Oxford: Blackwell, 1964), p. 157.

4. Mircea Eliade, *Birth and Rebirth: The Religious Meaning,* trans. Willard Trask (New York: Harper, 1958), p. 128.

5. *Ibid.*, p. 135.

6. Gibson Winter, *The New Creation as Metropolis* (New York: Macmillan, 1963), p. 127.

7. See John H. Elliott, *The Elect and the Holy* (Leiden: E. J. Brill, 1966).

8. Schmemann, p. 92.

9. *Ibid.*, p. 93.

10. Gustav Wingren, *Gospel and Church*, trans. Ross Mackenzie (Philadelphia: Fortress, 1964), pp. 53ff.

11. R. E. O. White, *The Biblical Doctrine of Initiation:*

A Theology of Baptism and Evangelism (Grand Rapids: Eerdmans, 1960), p. 127, n. 3.

12. Tertullian, *De Baptismo* 18; in E. C. Whitaker, *Documents of the Baptismal Liturgy*, 2nd ed. (London: S.P.C.K., 1970), p. 9.

13. Hippolytus, *The Apostolic Tradition* 17; Whitaker, p. 3.

14. This practice was already proposed in *Contemporary Worship 7: Holy Baptism*, Inter-Lutheran Commission on Worship, 1974, pp. 10–11. See also the rubrics and propers for a baptismal eucharist in *Lutheran Book of Worship*, Minister's Edition, pp. 188–89.

THE EUCHARIST AS WITNESS: THE WORLD AS SACRAMENT

1. J. G. Davies, *Worship and Mission* (London: SCM Press, 1966), p. 92.

2. Alexander Schmemann, *For the Life of the World* (St. Vladimir's Seminary Press, 1974), p. 15.

3. Louis Bouyer, *Rite and Man: Natural Sacredness and Christian Sacraments*, Eng. trans. (University of Notre Dame Press, 1963), p. 82.

4. Gibson Winter, *The New Creation as Metropolis* (New York: Macmillan, 1963), p. 100.

5. See Robert W. Jenson, Locus X, "The Means of Grace. Part Two: The Sacraments," in Carl E. Braaten and Robert W. Jenson, eds., *Christian Dogmatics*, II (Philadelphia: Fortress, 1984), 337ff.

6. See Frank C. Senn, arts. "Anamnesis" and "Epiclesis," in Peter E. Fink, S. J., ed., *The New Dictionary of Sacramental Worship* (Collegeville: The Liturgical Press, 1990), pp. 45f., 390f. See also the arts. by David N. Power, O.M.I., "The Anamnesis: Remembering, We Offer," and John H. McKenna, C. M., "The Epiclesis Revisited," in Frank C. Senn, ed., *New Eucharistic Prayers. An Ecumeni-*

cal Study of Their Development and Structure (New York and Mahwah: Paulist Press, 1987), pp. 146ff., 169ff.

7. See Acts 20:7–12 (perhaps suggesting the eucharist at the end of a Saturday all-night vigil); Ignatius of Antioch, *Philadelphians* 4; *Didache* 14; Justin Martyr, *Apology*, I, 67.

8. See Frank C. Senn, "Frequency of Reception of Communion," in *The New Dictionary of Sacramental Worship, op. cit.*, pp. 241ff.

9. See Mircea Eliade, *Cosmos and History: The Myth of the Eternal Return*, trans. Willard Trask (New York: Harper, 1959).

10. R. K. Orchard, *Mission in a Time of Testing* (Philadelphia: Westminster, 1964), p. 45.

11. Louis Bouyer, *Liturgical Piety* (University of Notre Dame Press, 1954), pp. 266ff.

12. Alexander Schmemann, "The Missionary Imperative in the Orthodox Tradition," in G. H. Anderson, ed., *The Theology of Christian Mission* (New York: McGraw-Hill, 1961), p. 256.

13. These are the five models of the church all based on biblical images and developed in Avery Dulles, S. J., *Models of the Church* (Garden City: Doubleday and Co., 1974).

14. See Joseph Jungmann, *The Mass of the Roman Rite: Its Origins and Development*, trans. Francis A. Brunner (Westminster, Md.: Christian Classics, 1986), II, 432ff.

INVITATIONAL EVANGELISM: HOSPITALITY AND INCULTURATION

1. Ben Johnson, *An Evangelism Primer: Practical Principles for Congregations* (Atlanta: John Knox Press, 1983), p. 33.

2. See Patrick Keifert, "Guess Who's Coming to Worship? Worship and Evangelism," *Word and World* IX

(1989), 46–51. These ideas have been developed and expanded in Patrick Keifert, *Welcoming the Stranger: A Public Theology of Worship and Evangelism* (Minneapolis: Fortress Press, 1991).

3. Willy Malarcher, "Hospitality," in Peter Fink, ed., *The New Dictionary of Sacramental Worship* (Collegeville: The Liturgical Press, 1990), pp. 558–62.

4. Victor Turner, "Passages, Margins, and Poverty: Religious Symbols of Communitas," *Worship* 46 (1972), 391.

5. See Aidan Kavanagh, *On Liturgical Theology* (New York: Pueblo Publishing Co, 1984), ch. 4: "Church Doing World," pp. 52–69.

6. Frank C. Senn, *Christian Worship and Its Cultural Setting* (Philadelphia: Fortress Press, 1983), p. 51.

7. Kenneth Smits, "Liturgical Reform in a Cultural Perspective," *Worship* 50 (1976), 98ff.

8. See Anscar J. Chupungco, *Cultural Adaptation of the Liturgy* (New York: Paulist Press, 1982).

9. G. A. Arbuckle, "Inculturation not Adaptation: Time to Change Terminology," *Worship* 60 (1986), 511–20.

10. See Peter Schineller, S. J., "Inculturation of the Liturgy," in *The New Dictionary of Sacramental Worship*, pp. 598–601.

11. *The Library of Christian Classics*, Vol. I. *Early Christian Fathers*, trans. and ed. Cyril C. Richardson (Philadelphia: The Westminster Press, 1953), p. 287.

12. See Gregory Dix, *The Shape of the Liturgy* (London: Dacre Press, 1945), pp. 36ff. on the synaxis, 103ff. on the eucharist.

13. See John L. Heinemeier, "Class or Mass: Some Thoughts on Black Lutheran Liturgy," *Lutheran Forum* 25/2 (1991), 32–34, for a model of how African-American elements have been integrated into the structure of the

Lutheran liturgy. A number of liturgical churches are finding the African-American Catholic Hymnal, *Lead Me,
Guide Me* (G.I.A. Publications), to be a useful resource.

14. See Mark R. Francis, C.S.V., *Liturgy in a Multicultural Community* (Collegeville: The Liturgical Press,
1991). On the specific challenge of Hispanic ministry see
Joseph Fitzgerald, *One Church Many Cultures: The Challenge of Diversity* (Kansas City: Sheed and Ward, 1987).

15. See Mary Collins, O.S.B., *Worship: Renewal to
Practice* (Washington: The Pastoral Press, 1987), pp.
197ff. on "Inclusive Language" and 215ff. "Naming God
in Public Prayer." Even though "Father" is a name of God
which Christians cannot avoid using in obedience to Jesus'
instruction, "When you pray say . . . ," this does not mean
that God is male and therefore the use of the pronoun "he"
when referring to God should be avoided as much as possible. See Gail Ramshaw-Schmidt, "De Divinis Nominibus:
The Gender of God," *Worship* 56 (1982), 129, and her
further discussion in *Christ in Sacred Speech* (Philadelphia: Fortress Press, 1986).

16. See Ignatius of Antioch, *Philadelphians* 4;
Smyrnaeans 8.

17. See G. G. Willis, *Further Essays in Early Roman Liturgy*. Alcuin Club Collections No. 50 (London: S.P.C.K.,
1968), pp. 4ff.; Theodore Klauser, *A Short History of the
Western Liturgy*, trans. John Halliburton (London: Oxford
University Press, 1969), pp. 59ff.

18. See J. D. C. Fisher, *Christian Initiation: Baptism in
the Medieval West* (London: S.P.C.K., 1965), pp. 52ff.;
also J. D. C. Fisher, *Confirmation Then and Now*. Alcuin
Club Collections No. 60 (London: S.P.C.K., 1978), pp.
126ff.

19. See Gerard Austin, *Anointing with the Spirit: The
Rite of Confirmation* (New York: Pueblo Publishing Co.,
1985), pp. 23ff. Aidan Kavanagh, *Confirmation: Origins*

and Reform (New York: Pueblo Publishing Co., 1988) argues that confirmation derives from the practice of solemn episcopal dismissals in the early liturgies, including the baptismal liturgy, and therefore has a modest origin which argues against making extravagant claims for the purpose of the rite. On the other hand, this rite, modest in origins, has served important pastoral and missionary needs during the course of its multifaceted evolution.

20. See Stephen Neill, *A History of Christian Missions.* The Pelican History of the Church: 6 (Penguin Books, 1964), especially pp. 61ff., 99ff.

WHEN THE PUBLIC COMES TO CHURCH: FESTIVALS AND OCCASIONAL SERVICES

1. *Service Book and Hymnal* of the Lutheran Church in America (Minneapolis: Augsburg Publishing House, *et al.,* 1958), #433; words by Emily E. S. Elliott (1836–97).

2. See John Koenig, *New Testament Hospitality: Partnership with Strangers as Promise and Mission* (Philadelphia: Fortress Press, 1985), pp. 26ff.

3. See Gerd Theissen, *The Social Setting of Pauline Christianity: Essays on Corinth,* ed. and trans. John H. Schutz (Philadelphia: Fortress Press, 1982), ch. 4: "Social Integration and Sacramental Activity: An Analysis of I Cor. 11:17–34," pp. 145ff.

4. See Gerald J. Hoffman, *How Your Congregation Can Become a More Hospitable Community* (Minneapolis: Augsburg Publishing House, 1990). This workbook for congregations should be used as a way of getting members to think about and work on their practices of hospitality, not as a legalistic prescription for membership recruitment. I would put suggestion #18 into the latter category: "Within 48 hours of a visit to the church, the visitor receives a personal contact from a member or a pastor of the

congregation thanking them for coming and inviting them to return" (pp. 18f.). It should be noted that this suggestion for "rushing" visitors into membership is derived from Win Arn, *The Win Arn Growth Report*, Institute for American Church Growth, Vol. 1. This suggestion could work against suggestion #13: "The reception of visitors communicates a sincere invitation into fellowship and at the same time respects privacy and allows anonymity" (p. 16). For further discussion of this delicate balancing act, see Roy M. Oswald and Speed B. Leas, *The Inviting Church: A Study of New Member Assimilation* (The Alban Institute, 1987), p. 52.

5. Anton Baumstark, *Comparative Liturgy*, English trans. (Westminster: Newman Press, 1958), p. 27.

6. See the discussion of traditions versus "The Tradition" in Paul Hoon, *The Integrity of Worship* (Nashville and New York: Abingdon Press, 1971), pp. 95–102.

7. From the Order for the Burial of the Dead, *Lutheran Book of Worship*, Pew Edition (Minneapolis: Augsburg Publishing House and Philadelphia: Board of Publication, Lutheran Church in America, 1978), p. 211.

8. Martin Luther, *The Small Catechism*, Part III; in *The Book of Concord*, ed. and trans. Theodore G. Tappert (Philadelphia: Fortress Press, 1959), pp. 346ff.

LITURGY AND EVANGELISM: CALENDAR COORDINATION

1. See *The Treatise on The Apostolic Tradition of St. Hippolytus of Rome*, ed. and trans. Gregory Dix (London: S.P.C.K., 1968).

2. See Edward J. Yarnold, *The Awe-inspiring Rites of Initiation: Baptismal Homilies of the Fourth Century* (New York: St. Paul Publications, 1972).

3. See E. C. Whitaker, *Documents of the Baptismal Liturgy* (London: S.P.C.K., 1970), pp. 166ff.

4. See J. D. C. Fisher, *Christian Initiation: Baptism in the Medieval West* (London: S.P.C.K., 1965).

5. See *The Rites of the Catholic Church as Revised by the Second Vatican Ecumenical Council* (New York: Pueblo Publishing Co., 1976), pp. 3ff.

6. *Ibid.*, p. 22.

7. See the symposium on the R.C.I.A. at Ten Years by Raymond Kemp, with responses by Mark Searle, Ralph A. Keifer, and James W. Fowler in *Worship* 56 (July 1982), 309–43.

8. Aidan Kavanagh, *The Shape of Baptism: The Rite of Christian Initiation* (New York: Pueblo Publishing Co., 1978), p. 127.

9. See Alfred McBride, O. Praem., *Invitation: The Search for God, Self and Church* (Washington, D.C.: Paulist National Catholic Evangelization Association, 1984).

10. *The Catechumenal Process: Adult Initiation and Formation for Christian Life and Ministry*, ed. Rev. Ann E. P. McElligott (New York: The Church Hymnal Corporation, 1990).

11. *Occasional Services: A Companion to Lutheran Book of Worship* (Minneapolis: Augsburg Publishing House, 1982), pp. 13ff.

12. On Integrating Affirmation of Baptism with Holy Baptism see Frank C. Senn, *The Pastor As Worship Leader* (Minneapolis: Augsburg Publishing House, 1977), pp. 74ff.

CHRISTIAN INITIATION: A TASK FOR THE TERRITORIAL CHURCH

1. Aidan Kavanagh, *The Shape of Baptism* (New York: Pueblo Publishing Co., 1978), p. 108.

2. *Ibid.*, p. 155.

3. See James A. Wilde, ed., *Before and After Baptism* (Chicago: Liturgy Training Publications, 1988); also Aidan

Kavanagh, "Unfinished and Unbegun Revisited: The Rite of Christian Initiation of Adults," *Worship* 53 (1979), pp. 327–40.

4. See Frank C. Senn, "Liturgy and Polity in the Ancient and Medieval Church: Lessons from History for a Church Renewed," *Currents in Theology and Mission* 12 (1985), pp. 220–31.

5. See Frederic van der Meer, *Augustine the Bishop*, trans. B. Battershaw and G. R. Lamb (London: Sheed and Ward, 1961), pp. 298 ff.

6. See the *Book of Concord*, ed. and trans. Theodore G. Tappert (Philadelphia: Fortress Press, 1959), pp. 337 ff. (Small Catechism), 357 ff. (Large Catechism).

7. See E. C. Whitaker, *Documents of the Baptismal Liturgy*, 2d ed. (London: S.P.C.K., 1970), pp. 172 ff.

8. See Robert Jenson, *A Large Catechism* (New York: American Lutheran Publicity Bureau, 1990); originally published as a series in *The Lutheran Forum.*

9. The ideas which follow were previously proposed by Frank C. Senn, "Preparing for the Greatest Feast," in *Rite Ideas.* Vol. 19, No. 2 (C.S.S. Publishing Co., 1990).

10. See the commentary on the Vigil readings in Philip Pfatteicher and Carlos Messerli, *Manual on the Liturgy: Lutheran Book of Worship* (Minneapolis: Augsburg Publishing House, 1979), pp. 331 ff.